Your Florida Guide to

SHRUBS

Your Florida Guide to

SHRUBS

Selection, Establishment and Maintenance

Edward F. Gilman

Robert J. Black

Florida Cooperative Extension Service
Institute of Food and Agricultural Sciences
University of Florida

University Press of Florida
Gainesville/Tallahassee/Tampa/Boca Raton/Pensacola/Orlando/Miami/Jacksonville

Gilman, Edward F.
Your Florida Guide to Shrubs: Selection, Establishment and Maintenance / Edward F. Gilman, Robert J. Black.
p. cm.
Includes index.
ISBN 0-8130-1673-8 (pbk.: alk. paper)
1. Ornamental shrubs--Florida. I. Black, Robert J. (Robert John), 1942- . II. Title. III. Title: Shrubs.
SB435.52.F6G55 1999
635.9'76'09759--dc21 98-31992

Designer: Katrina Vitkus
Editor: Sarah W. Miller

The Florida Cooperative Extension Service at the University of Florida's Institute of Food and Agricultural Sciences is a partnership of county, state and federal government which serves the citizens of Florida by providing information and training on a wide variety of topics. In Florida, the Extension Service is a part of the University of Florida's Institute of Food and Agricultural Sciences with selected programs at Florida Agricultural and Mechanical University (FAMU). Extension touches almost everyone in the state from the homeowner to huge agribusiness operations in such areas as: food safety, gardening, child and family development, consumer credit counseling, youth development, energy conservation, sustainable agriculture, competitiveness in world markets, and natural resource conservation.

The University Press of Florida is the scholarly publishing agency for the State University System of Florida, comprising Florida A&M University, Florida Atlantic University, Florida International University, Florida State University, University of Central Florida, University of Florida, University of North Florida, University of South Florida, and University of West Florida.

University Press of Florida
15 NW 15th Street
Gainesville, FL 32611-2079
http://www.upf.com

Table of Contents

Acknowledgments vi

Section 1

Getting started 2

Selecting and planting shrubs 4

Section 2

Shrub selection guide 24

Glossary 25

Section 3

Establishing and maintaining shrubs 84

Appendices 104

Index 108

Acknowledgments

Editor

Sarah W. Miller

Designer/illustrator

Katrina Vitkus

Photographers

Robert Black

Edward Gilman

Consultants

Diane Weigle

Proofreader

Carol Magary

Indexer

Carol Magary

Getting Started

It's Saturday morning, you're sipping your favorite beverage, the sun's coming up through the trees. You slowly look from one side of the yard to the other. Let's face it. The yard needs work! You want to screen off that undesirable view. You want to hide your neighbor's ugly fence. You want your house to sit in the landscape more comfortably instead of sticking out like a sore thumb. You've thought about hiring someone to design and install your vision of the yard for you, but you can't afford it. Your cousin says he can do it, but you don't trust him. So you decide to tackle the job yourself. This book guides you through the simple process of choosing appropriate shrubs to renew your landscape, and provides a reference for their care once they are planted. Although almost anyone can do a mediocre landscaping job with shrubs, by using this book you have made the decision to do it right this time.

Selecting and Planting Shrubs

Early considerations and planning

An environmentally sound landscape begins with a design based on a thorough evaluation of the site. Whether designing a new landscape or renovating an old one, low maintenance is often the primary concern (Figures 1a-b). A low-maintenance landscape not only saves time and money, but also conserves water and energy. Low-maintenance design is achieved through proper plant selection, as well as thoughtful arrangement of plants on the site. A low-maintenance design often combines existing native trees and shrubs into the landscape plan (Figure 2).

Unfortunately, many landscapes are poorly designed (Figures 3a-b). Often in a new subdivision the same plants are used everywhere, making all the yards look similar. Large-maturing shrubs, such as red-tip photinia, viburnums, privets, and pittosporum, are

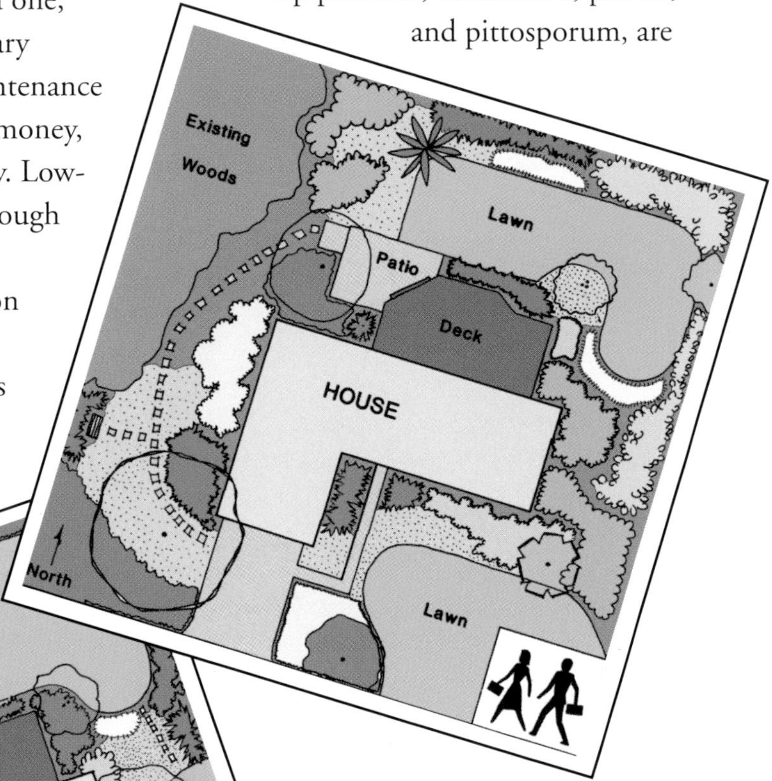

Figure 1a. This landscape (above) is designed with low maintenance in mind. The sizable portion of the existing woods left intact will require little maintenance. Large sections of the landscape are covered with shrub borders or ground covers that require regular but infrequent maintenance.

Figure 1b. This design (left) may be more suitable for the family with children because it has a larger lawn area for playing games.

Figure 2. In order to draw birds and other wildlife to the yard, and to save time in mowing and other maintenance, incorporate existing trees and shrubs into the landscape plan.

inappropriately placed in front of windows or too close to the house (Figures 4a-d, p. 10). This is usually because large plants of these species are relatively inexpensive. Instead of cramming plants up against the house, extend shrubs and ground covers away from the foundation. You can use common shrubs to develop a unique and different look to your yard. Consider using plants you are not yet familiar with but would enjoy having in your landscape.

While trees give landscape plantings important design elements of dimension, scale and profile, shrubs are scaled to

Figure 3a. *While looking neat and well-maintained now, the plants in this design (above) will quickly outgrow their allotted spaces. The Saw Palmetto in the foreground left will grow into and over the three small shrubs planted at the edge of the bed. The palm under the eave of the house will grow into the eave and will need to be removed. The small hedge in front of the bed against the house will need regular clipping to keep it looking neat. The shrubs on either side of the window require regular clipping to keep them from growing into the window and into the eave.*

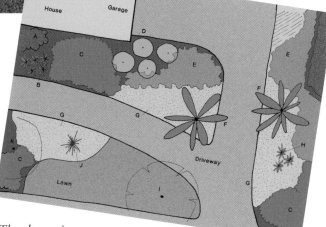

The alternative landscape design (above) represented in the plan view drawing will reduce maintenance requirements. These plants are smaller at maturity and grow at a slow or moderate pace, and there is less grass to mow. Lawn area is reduced to the small area near the street.

Table 1. Plant key for Figure 3a.

Area	Desired maximum height for the area	Suggested plants for		
		North Florida	Central Florida	South Florida
A	4-6 feet	gardenia	gardenia	pinwheel flower
B	2-3	African iris	African iris	bird-of-paradise
C	2-3	Indian hawthorn	Indian hawthorn	Indian hawthorn
D	6-8	rose-of-Sharon	rose-of-Sharon	hibiscus
E	2-3	parson's juniper	parson's juniper	parson's juniper
F	15-25	pindo palm	pindo palm	pindo palm
G	2	trailing lantana	trailing lantana	trailing lantana
H	2-4	variegated ginger	variegated ginger	ixora
I	25-40	yaupon holly	tree ligustrum	orchid-tree
J	6-8	Spanish bayonet	Spanish bayonet	Spanish bayonet
K	8-12	fringe tree	fringe tree	yellow poinciana

Table 2. Plant key for Figure 3b.

Area	Desired maximum height for the area	Suggested plants for North Florida	Central Florida	South Florida
A	4-6 feet	spirea	spirea	cardboard cycad
B	2-3	andorra juniper	parson's juniper	parson's juniper
C	1-2	trailing lantana	trailing lantana	trailing lantana
D	4-5	Formosa azalea	Formosa azalea	plumbago
E	4-5	ginger	ginger	ginger
F	>35	live oak	live oak	mahogany
G	8	podocarpus	podocarpus	podocarpus
H	2-3	Indian hawthorn	Indian hawthorn	Indian hawthorn
I	3-4	dwarf yaupon holly	dwarf yaupon holly	natal-plum (dwarf)
J	6-8	camellia	camellia	ixora
K	8-10	rose-of-Sharon	hibiscus	hibiscus
L	4-6	gardenia	gardenia	yellow butterfly palm
M	15-20	crape myrtle	crape myrtle	silver buttonwood
N	1-2	trailing lantana	trailing lantana	trailing lantana
O	30-40	nagi podocarpus	nagi podocarpus	nagi podocarpus
P	30-40	Chinese elm	Chinese elm	Chinese elm
Q	1-2	'Evergreen Giant' liriope	'Evergreen Giant' liriope	'Evergreen Giant' liriope

Figure 3b. Many landscapes in Florida look like the one pictured above. Shrubs are placed only along a narrow strip next to the foundation of the home. There is little choice but to prune them into balls or boxes because they are too close to the house.

The alternative landscape design represented in the plan view drawing (left) provides a welcoming lawn area surrounded by an array of trees, shrubs and ground covers. This creates a nice entry to the home and provides some privacy from the street.

Figure 3c. This design is very simple but provides an elegance not seen in many landscapes. The lawn area is ample and surrounded by ground covers and shrubs.

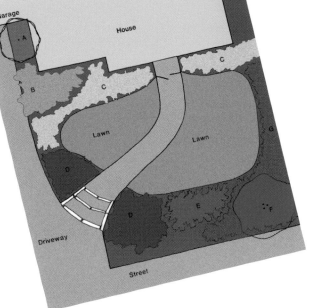

human size and eye level and thus provide balance, proportion and unity. To fully appreciate the role shrubs can play in your landscape, imagine them as part of an outdoor living area. In this scheme of things, trees provide the framework and overhead cover, turfgrass and other ground covers are the flooring, and shrubs form the walls, internal dividers and decoration (Figures 5a-c). They usually provide the best aesthetics when planted in groups of the same species.

		Table 3. Plant key for Figure 3c.		
	Desired maximum height	Suggested plants for		
Area	for the area	North Florida	Central Florida	South Florida*
A	25 feet	dahoon holly	East Palatka holly	tabebuia
B	6-8	anise	anise	selloum
C	2	trailing lantana	trailing lantana	trailing lantana
D	3	lantana	lantana	Boston fern
E	1-2	dwarf procumbens juniper	dwarf procumbens juniper	leather fern
F	30-40	southern magnolia	loblolly bay	Queen's crape myrtle
G	2-4	coontie	coontie	cardboard cycad

*This landscape was photographed in south Florida. Substitute the suggested plants for north and central Florida.

Table 4. Plant key for Figure 3d.

Area	Desired maximum height for the area	North Florida*	Central Florida	South Florida
		Suggested plants for		
A	6-8 feet	round-leaf hawthorn	round-leaf hawthorn	round-leaf hawthorn
B	2-3	kurume azalea (dwarf)	dwarf pittosporum	pineapple
C	1	blue rug juniper	blue rug juniper	trailing lantana
D	10	fragrant osmanthus	fragrant osmanthus	lady palm
E	2-3	Indian hawthorn	Indian hawthorn	dwarf gamma grass
F	15-20	crape myrtle	crape myrtle	princess flower
G	10-15	anise	anise	sweet viburnum
H	>40	sugarberry	sugarberry	gumbo-limbo
I	4-5	blue vase juniper	blue vase juniper	scaevola
J	1-2	blue rug juniper	blue rug juniper	trailing lantana
K	3-4	saw palmetto	saw palmetto	saw palmetto
L	>30	live oak	live oak	pitchapple

* This landscape was photographed in north Florida. Substitute the suggested plants for central and south Florida.

Figure 3d. Notice the ample use of small shrubs and ground covers in this more developed design. As a result, little pruning will be required to maintain this landscape.

Figure 4a. Placing large shrubs such as Ligustrum (privet) too close to the house means that you will be clipping them regularly to keep them clear of the windows.

Figure 4b. Most of the shrubs in this landscape grow to a large size so they need regular pruning to keep them at the desired size. Some have grown so large that they are hiding the house.

Figure 4c. These shrubs are too large and are jammed against the house. The side of the house is completely hidden from view. Why create work for yourself with this type of design?

Figure 4d. There are too many different types of plants, and too many plants, in this small area. Constant maintenance is required to keep this landscape looking tidy. Four or five different types would have been adequate, and about half as many nursery plants needed to be installed.

Figure 5a. A modest lawn area surrounded by ground covers and shrubs makes a nice front- or backyard display.

Figure 5b. Group or mass several plants of the same species together instead of placing them separately. Intersperse shrub areas with lower ground covers and trees.

Figure 5c. A plant grouping or border can be used to screen an undesirable view. This often looks better than a hedge and is easy to maintain.

Although the plants and designs may differ, all landscapes perform the same important functions. A well-planned landscape enhances the beauty of a home and moderates the climate around it by protecting it from extremes of wind, heat, cold and glare. Healthy landscape plants minimize the amount of rainwater runoff and sediments reaching streams and storm sewers. Shrubs can decorate a deck or patio area (Figure 6). Furthermore, landscaping can increase a home's value by 15 percent and reduce home cooling costs by 30 percent.

For your planting scheme to be a success, select a healthy plant that is the

Figure 6. Small shrubs make nice potted plants for use on a deck or patio.

right size and species for its place in the landscape and one that harmonizes with neighboring plants and buildings. You will also need to see that the shrub is properly planted and established, so that it becomes a healthy and beautiful addition to your landscape.

Figure 7a. The layout of beds in the landscape can be made easily with a garden hose.

Figure 7b. Use the hose to experiment with different shapes for beds or borders.

Bed design and preparation

Start your bed and border designs with sketches and make your mistakes on paper, not on the landscape site. Sample plans and designs are presented in Figures 3c-d, 4a-d, and 5a-c. The shape of the beds will greatly influence the character of your landscape. Beds and borders with straight lines can be monotonous because they are repeated in walks, drives and property lines. However, when the rest of the yard is composed of straight lines, they can be used successfully. Curved or moderately free-flowing designs are restful to the eye and create a relaxing, progressive, moving and natural feeling that contributes to the informal effect.

After you have determined the size and shape of your beds and borders, they can be laid out in the landscape with the help of a garden hose (Figures 7a-b). Simply outline

Your Florida Guide to Shrubs

Figure 8a. Start removing grass or other plants inside the bed by digging along the inside edge of the hose, defining the outer edge of the bed.

Figure 8b. An efficient method of removing the remaining sod is to make vertical cuts around small sections of turf and then push the shovel horizontally under the sod to loosen.

Figure 8c. Once the sod has been loosened, it can be removed in pieces and stacked in a wheelbarrow for easy transplanting or composting.

Figure 8d. When the bed area has been cleared of all sod, it is ready for additional preparation prior to planting.

Figure 8e. Once all grass is removed, you are ready to choose appropriate plants.

the shapes of the beds and borders on the ground with a flexible hose and dig and remove grass or other plants inside the outlined area (Figures 8a-e).

Selecting the appropriate shrubs for your landscape

Climatic considerations

To obtain the most satisfactory landscape effects, shrubs should be adapted to the environment in which they are to be planted. In general, the northern areas of Florida are subject to frequent heavy frosts and freezes, whereas southern Florida rarely experiences frosts. Because of such differences in winter temperatures throughout the state, comparatively few shrubs are adapted for statewide use.

There are no clear lines of demarcation between the major climatic zones in the state. However, Florida can be roughly divided into northern (hardiness zone 8), central (hardiness zone 9) and southern zones (hardiness zones 10 and 11). A given landscape or portion of it may be a few degrees warmer or cooler than the rest of the climatic zone because of the site's proximity to a lake or coast, its elevation, or its air drainage. (Air drainage refers to the phenomenon of cold air moving down a slope to settle in the lowest area in the landscape.) As a consequence of such variables, a landscape might accommodate plants that are not usually recommended for its hardiness zone. The hardiness map (Figure 9) can be used as a guide for selecting shrubs that will survive the cold temperatures expected in your area of the state. It also can be used to indicate how far south a shrub will grow. The hardiness-zone range given for each shrub indicates the coldest (smallest zone number) and warmest (largest zone number) areas of the state where that plant will grow well. For example, firebush grows well in zones 9A (central Florida) through 11 (the Florida Keys).

On the basis of response to cold temperatures, shrubs may be classified as "tender," "semi-hardy" or "hardy" in each of the three climatic zones of the state. A plant considered hardy in south Florida might be considered tender in north Florida. Adapted hardy plants can be grown throughout northern Florida. Some semi-hardy plants grown in central Florida can be successfully grown in warmer parts of northern peninsular Florida. Shrubs located in regions colder than indicated by their hardiness-zone range may be killed to the ground some years, but often come back from the roots in the spring. For example, princess-flower will be killed to the ground in the winter in north Florida, but new growth emerges in the spring. Subject to this die-back, these shrubs will not reach their mature size and might be grown as perennials reaching 4 to 6 feet tall each year. Tender plants are confined largely to southern Florida, but a few species are adapted to the warmest parts of central Florida. Semi-hardy and tender plants will normally survive lower temperatures when mature, or if they have been previously conditioned by several weeks of cool or cold temperatures prior to a freeze. At the other extreme, some shrubs require specified periods of cool or cold temperatures to induce dormancy required for proper growth and flowering in the next season.

match the light level, soil, and other characteristics of the site. These characteristics can differ greatly within the same landscape. In a landscape that contains large trees, light levels can vary in different areas of the site from full sun exposure to dense shade. In some regions of the state, soil can vary from well-drained sand to poorly drained clay.

Most shrubs are well-adapted to a wide range of soil types, soil moisture conditions and pH ranges, but most grow best in slightly acid to neutral soils (pH of 5.5 to 7). If your soil pH is above 7.5, choose shrubs tolerant of alkaline soil. If you ignore this advice, you risk increasing maintenance costs due to pH-induced nutrient deficiencies. Although some shrubs tolerate dry, sandy soils and some tolerate poorly drained soils, most grow best in moist, well-drained soils. Most shrubs adapted to well-drained soils do not grow well if soil remains wet. Shrubs

Figure 9. Know the hardiness zone of your location before selecting shrubs for the landscape.

Environmental and other considerations

Before heading to a nursery, study the environmental conditions of your landscape site. The time you spend doing this now will pay dividends in healthy plants, lower maintenance costs, and fewer plant replacements in the future. Plants have different requirements, and the success of planting depends on how well you select shrubs that

Figure 10a. Using too much colorful foliage can be distracting.

Figure 10b. Use color in moderation to obtain pleasing designs.

adapted to moist soils usually grow poorly in dry, sandy locations. Those adapted to flooding or poorly drained soils are the best choices for areas of the yard where water accumulates. If you dig a planting hole and it fills with water, or water runs into the bottom of the hole from the sides, be sure

that the shrub you chose to plant tolerates wet soil.

Some people prefer to plant only Florida native shrubs in their yard. Fortunately, many garden centers and nurseries offer these well-adapted plants. The Shrub

Selection Guide (p. 24) will indicate for each shrub whether it is native to the state of Florida. There is also a list of native shrubs in Appendix 6. Shrubs can also be chosen on the basis of plant architecture (form, texture, color and size) and availability. Frequently, undue emphasis is given to plants that have striking characteristics such as an unusual color. Although plants producing striking effects may be put to good use in the landscape, they should be used sparingly, and their location should be carefully chosen (Figures 10a-b).

Determine plant sizes and numbers

Choose the appropriate mature plant size for the site. Although a shrub may look small in the nursery, it can rapidly outgrow its allotted area after a few years. Consider its final mature height and spread, as well as how long it will take to reach that size. Often,

dwarf varieties of shrubs are good choices for sites next to buildings, driveways and roads. You don't need to prune these plants frequently and, because dwarf plants stay small, you won't have to replace them for outgrowing their space. Unfortunately, most people choose large-maturing shrubs inadvertently. Because these grow the fastest in the nursery, they can be purchased in a large size for a relatively low price. However, you will pay many, many times the original cost

Figure 11a. Unless a hedge is desired, designs with shrubs spaced too close together waste money, increase disease incidence and pruning requirement, and can form an unattractive mass of plants.

Figure 11b. Shrubs spaced farther apart form a more natural, open shape.

of the shrub when you have to prune it to keep it in bounds. Most homeowners and landscape designers could construct more efficient landscapes by increasing the use of low-growing shrubs and ground covers, and using less of those that require pruning to keep them at the desired height.

Unless planting a hedge, base the number of plants you need on the mature spread of the plant, the space to be planted, the growth rate, and the planting density you desire (Figures 11a-b). In areas where you want a mass effect — such as a hedge — shrubs can be planted close together. In most other instances, space them far enough apart to allow each to develop its natural form or shape. This provides a softer effect in the landscape, reduces pruning requirement, and can minimize disease problems by providing good air circulation within the shrub canopy.

Examine shrubs at the nursery

After deciding the kind and number of shrubs you need, you are ready to shop for reasonably priced, good-quality plants. Healthy ones establish faster and have fewer problems than plants in poor health. That is why it is so important that you examine them very closely and look for healthy, vigorous ones. A plant kept in its container too long is often larger than others and has roots wrapping around the inside of the container. It is likely to grow slowly once it is planted. Therefore, when choosing among shrubs in a given container size it is often best to choose the moderately sized shrubs, not the largest ones.

Avoid plants that are infested with lacebugs, spider mites, whiteflies or scales. These pests suck juices from leaves and stems and can seriously damage a plant. They can also spread to existing plants in your landscape. Some of these pests are very small and are only visible through a magnifying lens. You can easily detect their damage to plant foliage, which often manifests itself as flecking or spotting on the uppersides of leaves. Spotted leaves also can be a symptom of a leaf-spot disease. Except for Indian hawthorn, red-tip photinia and some other shrubs, this disease is not usually serious, but you are better off buying disease-free plants.

Inspect for mechanical injury

Inspect plants closely, and don't purchase any with scars or open wounds along their stems. Large pruning wounds are unsightly and expose the shrub to a higher incidence of decay.

Don't buy shrubs with many broken branches or torn leaves. A plant with a few small, broken twigs is acceptable if they can be removed without destroying the plant's shape. Removal of large branches results in large holes in the plant's canopy, and it could take years for the plant to regain its natural shape.

Examine grafted plants, such as gardenia, to determine if the graft union has closed properly. The union is typically close to the ground and should be smooth and clean. There should be no suckers on the stem below the graft union.

Check for cold injury

Stems and roots may be damaged on tender shrubs that were left unprotected from frost or freezing temperatures. Obvious cold-injury symptoms are brown leaves, split bark, dead branches, and brown roots. Some plants may not express cold injury symptoms until they are stressed by warmer weather in the spring or summer. Therefore, if you are buying plants after an unusually cold winter, you should closely inspect their

roots and stems in the spring or summer for signs of root injury or split bark.

Study condition and shape of canopy

Select specimens with uniform canopies densely filled to the ground with healthy, vigorous leaves of normal size, shape, color and texture. Young shrubs or those spaced too closely together in the nursery may not develop a uniform canopy until placed in the landscape for several years. Avoid plants with leaves of abnormal size or excessively yellowed leaves unless the plant naturally has variegated or multicolored foliage. High-quality large plants have stems that are well-formed and sturdy, with plenty of uniformly distributed branches forming a well-balanced plant. Unevenly spaced branches or branches clustered together on the main stem usually result in weak or leggy plants, which you should avoid.

Examine the root system

Don't look only at the above-ground parts of a plant because its ultimate survival depends largely on the health of its root system. For this reason, buy your plants from a nursery that allows customers to examine the roots of the plants. Shrubs purchased from nurseries usually come in containers. Occasionally, some are offered balled and burlapped. Inspect the roots of a container-grown plant by laying it on its side and sliding the container off the root ball. If you find it difficult to remove the container, the plant may be root-bound (Figure 12a). Root-bound plants have a mass of roots circling the outside surface of the root ball. This root mass can be so dense that it prevents roots from penetrating the soil after planting. Circling roots can also girdle the plant as it grows and eventually kill it. On the other hand, if the

Figure 12a. Pot-bound (root-bound) plant.

Figure 12b. Recently repotted plant.

root ball falls apart (Figure 12b) when you remove the container, it could have been repotted recently or the root system may be inadequate or unhealthy. You could be buying a container of potting media with very few roots.

Examine the roots on the surface of the root ball. Don't buy a plant with mushy, dark brown or black roots (Figure 12c).

These roots were probably killed by heat stress, freezing temperatures, overwatering or drought. Poke your finger into the rooting medium next to the main trunk to look and feel for bent or circling roots. These can prevent shrubs from becoming established properly and can lead to premature plant death.

Roots should be distributed throughout the container medium. They should not protrude outside the container or penetrate the ground (Figure 12d). If you try to pick up a container plant and find it is fastened to the ground by escaping roots, move to another plant. The root ball should be free of weeds (Figure 12e). Weeds will slow the establishment rate of a plant and may spread into the surrounding landscape. The root ball should be moist, not dry, and you should see some whitish, yellow or light brown roots on the sides of the root ball when you slip it from the container.

The root balls of plants balled and burlapped should be moist, with the soil firmly held around the roots by burlap that has been tightly secured with pins, twine or wire. The stem of the plant should be sturdy in the root ball. A loose or droopy root ball indicates that the plant was treated roughly and may result in poor plant establishment and growth in the landscape.

Figure 12c. Plant with black roots on root ball.

Figure 12d. Plant with escaping roots.

Planting shrubs

When to plant

Shrubs can be planted throughout the year in Florida. If regular irrigation is not available, plant in late May or June when the rainy season normally begins, and plant small shrubs. Shrubs larger than the 3-gallon size could easily die from too little water unless irrigation is supplied regularly until established.

Figure 12e. Plant with obvious weed problem.

Handling and preparing root balls for planting

If shrubs are to survive and become established in a landscape, they have to be handled and installed correctly. Root balls in containers are more resistant to rough handling than those balled and burlapped. A balled and burlapped plant should be handled carefully, because shifting of soil inside the root ball may break roots and leave cracks in the root ball. A cracked root ball will dry out more quickly and, therefore, require more water.

Before planting a container-grown shrub, slip the container off the root ball. The root ball should remain intact and be somewhat pliant (flexible). If the plant is root-bound or has many circling roots, you should slice the sides of the root ball with pruning shears, a serrated knife, or a utility knife. Make three or four evenly spaced slices, each one going from the top to the bottom of the root ball 1 to 2 inches deep. Any circling roots that remain should be pulled away from the root ball.

When planting a balled and burlapped plant, it is important to know whether the root ball is wrapped in natural or synthetic burlap. You can determine which type was used by holding a match to a small portion of the burlap. As a rule, natural burlap will burn, synthetic will melt. Because synthetic burlap does not decompose in the soil and can girdle roots, it must be entirely re-moved after the plant is placed in the planting hole. To do this, cut the string and ties from around the trunk, pull the burlap away from the sides of the root ball, tip the root ball to one side and push the burlap underneath it as far as possible. Then tip the root ball to the other side and slide the burlap out from under it. The tipping should be performed by handling only the root ball. Pushing or pulling on the trunk could crack the root ball. Natural burlap decomposes readily in the soil and can be left along the sides and bottom of the root ball, but should always be removed from the top of the root ball where it is subject to drying out. Dry burlap repels water, making it difficult to re-wet the root ball. **Always remove nylon twine used to hold burlap around the plant stem. Nylon twine does not rot and will eventually girdle the stem if left in place.**

Digging and filling the planting hole

Begin planting by digging the planting hole two to three times the diameter of the root ball (Figures 13a-b). The planting hole should never be dug any deeper than the height of the root ball. Disturbing the soil

Figure 13a. *Planting a shrub in well-drained soil.*

Figure 13b. *Planting a shrub in compacted or poorly drained soil.*

beneath the plant may cause it to settle too deep in the soil. Gently place the plant straight in the hole, making sure that the top of the root ball is not deeper than the surface of the surrounding soil. In compacted or poorly drained soil, the top quarter to top third of the root ball should be planted slightly above the soil surface with soil or mulch then placed around the exposed portion of the root ball to provide an adequate volume of well-drained soil for root development (Figure 13b).

After placing the root ball into the planting hole, backfill the bottom half of planting hole with loose, unamended soil. Mixing amendments such as organic matter or other soil conditioners into the backfill soil provides no benefit. Tamp the soil to settle it around the root ball, but not so heavily as to compact the soil. Finish filling the hole and gently tamp again. Instead of tamping lightly with your feet, you can settle the soil by moving a hose of running water up and down in the backfill soil all the way around the hole. Never place soil over the top of the root ball as this can prevent water from reaching the roots in the root ball, which can kill the shrub. Planting too deep and placing soil over the top of the root ball are among the leading causes of plant decline in many landscapes.

Sometimes the effects of planting too deep won't be seen for several years.

Construct a 2- to 3-inch-high soil berm (also called a water ring) around the outer edge of the root ball to hold irrigation water during the first growing season (Figures 13a-b). The 2- to 3-inch-high berm can also be constructed with mulch instead of soil. Never construct a berm or ring more than 3 inches high because this buries roots too deep and can lead to poor growth or plant mortality. By the end of the first growing season, remove the berm by pulling it away from the plant. Some roots will have grown well beyond the berm by then. Soil and mulch should never be pushed in against the trunk because this can bury the trunk, causing it to rot.

Planting shrubs in beds or as a hedge

If no trees or mature shrubs are in the vicinity, prepare the bed for a group or row of shrubs by spading or tilling the entire bed to a depth of 8 to 12 inches. If existing shrubs or trees are present nearby, keep spading or tilling activities outside their drip lines to avoid injuring their roots. Do not spade or till within the drip line of a tree — simply dig a hole for each shrub.

There may be some benefit to amending the soil in an entire bed with peat, compost or other organic soil amendments. Some researchers have found greater root growth in amended beds. If using soil amendments, spade or till 3 to 6 inches of organic matter such as compost into the

Figure 14a. *Spade or till organic matter and fertilizer into the bed to a depth of 6 to 12 inches.*

Figure 14b. *Level the soil in the bed with a garden rake.*

top 6 to 12 inches of soil in the entire planting bed prior to planting (Figures 14a-b). Then dig a hole for each shrub and backfill with the amended bed soil.

Mulching

Mulches (Table 5) enhance root growth, reduce soil temperature fluctuations, prevent packing and crusting of the soil, minimize runoff and soil erosion, conserve moisture, help control weeds, and add to the beauty of the landscape by providing a cover of uniform color and an interesting texture to the surface. Mulch newly planted shrubs with a 3-inch layer of organic or inorganic material. Keep the mulch 2 to 3 inches away from the stems of the plants. When placed against the stem, the high-moisture environment of the mulch increases the chances of stem rot, which can result in plant death.

When mulching an individual shrub planted in the lawn, cover an area at least two times wider than the planting hole. This will help the plant to establish more quickly by reducing competition from turfgrass. When mulching a shrub bed, cover the entire area of the bed.

Table 5: Mulches

Mulch type	Color	Longevity	Weed control	Notes
pine bark chips	dark brown	medium/long	good	acid-forming
pine needles	light brown	short	fair	acid-forming
cypress	light tan	long	very good	acid-forming (not recommended)
hardwood chips	brown/gray	medium/long	good	acid-forming
pine wood chips	tan	medium	good	acid-forming
oak leaves	dark/brown	short	fair/good	acid-forming (can blow around)
grass clippings	green	very short	good	mats down (not recommended)
yard debris	light brown	medium	fair	recycles yard waste (highly recommended)

Shrub Selection Guide

This section is a guide to help you select the right shrubs for your landscape, as well as a reference for care and maintenance of the plants once they are established. The plants are arranged in alphabetical order by scientific name. Consult the index for common names. Refer to the hardiness-zone map below to determine if a plant is suitable for your region of the state. Some terms used in Section II may be unfamiliar to you. Here is a short glossary of terms to help you through this section.

The state can be divided into hardiness zones indicated by numbers on this map. Each zone is divided into A (the cooler part of the zone) and B (the warmer part of the zone).

Glossary

Attracts butterflies/hummingbirds - a plant that attracts butterflies and/or hummingbirds because of its flowers or foliage.

Drought sensitive - a plant that withers and dies back or drops leaves during an extended dry period.

Established shrubs - newly planted shrubs whose roots have grown out of their root balls and into the surrounding soil. The moisture requirements of these plants are met by natural rainfall, except in dry weather or drought. The average time for a shrub planted from a 1-gallon container to become established is 3 months. For shrubs planted from 7-gallon containers, the average establishment period is 1 year.

Foundation - appropriate for planting along the foundation of a building to visually soften corners, sharp angles, and exposed high foundations.

Full sun - requires full sun to grow and/or flower properly.

Full sun to part shade - grows equally well in full sun or filtered shade.

High salt tolerance - can tolerate conditions on an ocean or gulf side of a beachfront building.

Invasive potential - plant could seed itself into nearby landscapes or woodlands; could reproduce in natural plant communities on conservation lands.

Mass planting - a method of planting where shrubs, usually of the same species, are planted close together to create a visual mass effect.

Mature size - the height that a shrub can be expected to attain in about 10 years.

Moderate salt tolerance - can be grown on the protected side of an ocean front building, but is often injured by salt-laden winds during a storm.

Mostly sunny - grows well in full sun during the morning, but benefits from some shade during hot afternoons.

Native plant - a plant considered indigenous to Florida.

Part shade to full shade - grows poorly in locations that receive full sun all day.

Tolerates drought - needs no supplemental irrigation once established.

Tolerates moderate drought - once established, only requires irrigation during a severe drought.

Tolerates poor drainage - can grow in soil that remains wet for several days after a heavy rain. Shrubs without this designation usually grow best in well-drained soil.

Botanical name: *Abelia* x *grandiflora*
Common name: Glossy Abelia
Hardiness zones: 5A-9B
Uses: mass planting; screen; attracts butterflies
Florida native: no
Plant type: evergreen shrub
Mature size: 6-8 feet tall and wide
Flower: pink and white, showy in spring, summer, fall
Light requirement: full sun to part shade
Soil pH tolerance: acid to slightly alkaline
Soil moisture: tolerates moderate drought
Salt tolerance: moderate
Notes: this species grows quickly; variegated and dwarf cultivars available; often pruned into a hedge, but poorly suited for this purpose

Botanical name: *Acalypha hispida*
Common name: Chenille Plant
Hardiness zones: 10A-11
Uses: container or planter; foundation; mass planting; accent
Florida native: no
Plant type: evergreen shrub
Mature size: 6-10 feet tall by 8 feet wide
Flower: red, showy year-round
Light requirement: full sun to part shade
Soil pH tolerance: acid to slightly alkaline
Soil moisture: tolerates moderate drought
Salt tolerance: moderate
Notes: beautiful plant with bright red flowers year-round

Botanical name: *Acalypha wilkesiana*
Common name: Copperleaf, Jacob's Coat
Hardiness zones: 10B-11
Uses: foundation; mass planting; container or planter; accent
Florida native: no
Plant type: evergreen shrub
Mature size: 8-12 feet tall and wide
Flower: inconspicuous in summer
Light requirement: full sun to part shade
Soil pH tolerance: acid to slightly alkaline
Soil moisture: tolerates poor drainage; likes ample moisture
Salt tolerance: moderate
Notes: grown for showy, copper-red foliage

Botanical name: *Acrostichum daneifolium*
Common name: Leather Fern
Hardiness zones: 9A-11
Uses: mass planting; accent; border
Florida native: yes
Plant type: evergreen, perennial fern
Mature size: 4-8 feet tall by 4-6 feet wide
Flower: none
Light requirement: full sun (if near or in water) to full shade
Soil pH tolerance: acid to slightly alkaline
Soil moisture: tolerates poor drainage; likes moist or flooded soil
Salt tolerance: high
Notes: large fern for a wet location in landscape

Botanical name: *Agave americana*
Common name: Century Plant
Hardiness zones: 8B-11
Uses: border; accent; mass planting
Florida native: no
Plant type: evergreen shrub
Mature size: 6-8 feet tall by 6-10 feet wide
Flower: white flowers are borne once on a 15- to 25-foot-tall stalk, then the plant dies
Light requirement: full sun to part shade
Soil pH tolerance: acid to alkaline
Soil moisture: tolerates extended drought
Salt tolerance: high
Notes: may flower 10-20 years after planting; leaves have sharp spine at the tip

Botanical name: *Agave angustifolia* 'Marginata'
Common name: Variegated Caribbean Agave
Hardiness zones: 10A-11
Uses: border; accent; mass planting
Florida native: no
Plant type: evergreen shrub
Mature size: 3-4 feet tall and wide
Flower: white flowers are borne once on a 15- to 25-foot-tall stalk, then the plant dies
Light requirement: full sun to part shade
Soil pH tolerance: acid to alkaline
Soil moisture: tolerates extended drought
Salt tolerance: high
Notes: nice accent in ground cover bed; leaves have sharp spine at the tip

Botanical name: *Allamanda neriifolia*
Common name: Bush Allamanda
Hardiness zones: 10B-11
Uses: accent; container or planter; foundation; border; hedge
Florida native: no
Plant type: viny, evergreen shrub
Mature size: 5-10 feet tall by 6-8 feet wide
Flower: bright yellow, showy in summer/fall
Light requirement: full sun to part shade
Soil pH tolerance: acid to alkaline
Soil moisture: tolerates extended drought
Salt tolerance: moderate
Notes: covered with bright flowers during warm season; can be maintained as a hedge with regular clipping

Botanical name: *Alpinia zerumbet* 'Variegata'
Common name: Variegated Shellflower, Variegated Shell Ginger
Hardiness zones: 9A-11
Uses: container or planter; border; mass planting; accent; indoors
Florida native: no   **Plant type:** perennial
Mature size: 3-7 feet tall by 5-6 feet wide
Flower: whitish flowers are produced periodically throughout the year
Light requirement: full sun to part shade
Soil pH tolerance: acid to slightly alkaline
Soil moisture: tolerates moderate drought and poor drainage
Salt tolerance: moderate
Notes: killed to ground during winter in north Florida, but comes back from roots in spring

Botanical name: *Ardisia escallonioides*
Common name: Marlberry
Hardiness zones: 10A-11
Uses: hedge; screen; attracts butterflies; border; small tree
Florida native: yes
Plant type: large, evergreen shrub or tree
Mature size: 12-20 feet tall by 6-10 feet wide
Flower: produces showy flowers periodically
Light requirement: full sun to part shade
Soil pH tolerance: acid to alkaline
Soil moisture: tolerates moderate drought
Salt tolerance: high
Notes: good as dense screen, or as small tree for small space

Botanical name: *Aucuba japonica*
Common name: Aucuba, Japanese Aucuba
Hardiness zones: 7B-10A
Uses: border; mass planting; container or planter; foundation; cut foliage/twigs; accent; house plant
Florida native: no
Plant type: evergreen shrub
Mature size: 4-8 feet tall by 3-4 feet wide
Flower: inconspicuous; greenish
Light requirement: mostly shaded to full shade
Soil pH tolerance: acid to slightly alkaline
Soil moisture: drought sensitive
Salt tolerance: low
Notes: variegated cultivar is very popular; provide regular fertilizer for vigorous growth; grows very slowly

Botanical name: *Berberis julianae*
Common name: Wintergreen Barberry
Hardiness zones: 6A-9A
Uses: foundation; hedge; border; screen
Florida native: no
Plant type: evergreen shrub
Mature size: 4-8 feet tall by 5 feet wide
Flower: showy white in spring
Light requirement: full sun to part shade
Soil pH tolerance: acid to slightly alkaline
Soil moisture: tolerates moderate drought
Salt tolerance: moderate
Notes: great barrier due to thorny foliage

Botanical name: *Berberis thunbergii*
Common name: Japanese Barberry
Hardiness zones: 4A-9A
Uses: foundation; border; mass planting; ground cover; hedge; edging
Florida native: no
Plant type: evergreen shrub
Mature size: 2-8 feet tall by 4-6 feet wide
Flower: inconspicuous; white
Light requirement: full sun to part shade
Soil pH tolerance: acid to alkaline
Soil moisture: tolerates moderate drought
Salt tolerance: low
Notes: dwarf selections make nice ground covers; cultivars available with either green or purple foliage

Notes: often grown in containers in north Florida and brought under cover in cold weather; thorny branches; dwarf cultivars make nice ground covers.

Botanical name: *Bougainvillea* spp.
Common name: Bougainvillea
Hardiness zones: 9B-11
Uses: container or planter; mass planting; espalier; hanging basket; cascades down a wall
Florida native: no
Plant type: viny, evergreen shrub
Mature size: can grow 30 feet or more on a trellis
Flower: red, orange, pink, white; showy year-round
Light requirement: full sun for best flowers
Soil pH tolerance: acid to slightly alkaline
Soil moisture: tolerates drought
Salt tolerance: moderate

Botanical name: *Breynia disticha*
Common name: Snowbush
Hardiness zones: 10A-11
Uses: accent; hedge; mass planting; cascades down a wall
Florida native: no
Plant type: viny, evergreen shrub
Mature size: 5-8 feet tall by 4-7 feet wide
Flower: white; showy in summer, fall
Light requirement: full sun to part shade
Soil pH tolerance: acid to slightly alkaline
Soil moisture: tolerates moderate drought
Salt tolerance: low
Notes: dwarf cultivar available at selected nurseries; white and red new foliage makes this a popular plant

Botanical name: *Brugmansia* spp.
Common name: Angel's Trumpet-Tree
Hardiness zones: 10A-11
Uses: container or planter; accent; perennial border
Florida native: no **Plant type:** evergreen shrub
Mature size: 8-14 feet tall by 10-15 feet wide
Flower: orange to creamy yellow; showy in spring, summer, fall
Light requirement: full sun to part shade
Soil pH tolerance: acid to slightly alkaline
Soil moisture: drought sensitive
Salt tolerance: low
Notes: striking flowers make this a popular accent plant; used as perennial in north and central Florida; seeds germinate in the landscape and could become weedy

Botanical name: *Brunfelsia grandiflora*
Common name: Yesterday-Today-and-Tomorrow
Hardiness zones: 9B-11
Uses: container or planter; accent; perennial border; foundation; mass planting
Florida native: no
Plant type: evergreen shrub
Mature size: 7-10 feet tall by 5-8 feet wide
Flower: blue and pink; showy in spring, summer, fall
Light requirement: full sun to part shade
Soil pH tolerance: acid to slightly alkaline
Soil moisture: tolerates moderate drought
Salt tolerance: moderate
Notes: flowers cover plant nearly year-round; flowers change colors over two days, then fade

Botanical name: *Buddleia* spp.
Common name: Butterfly-Bush
Hardiness zones: 6A-10B
Uses: container or planter; accent; perennial border; attracts butterflies/hummingbirds
Florida native: no
Plant type: deciduous shrub
Mature size: 6-12 feet tall and wide
Flower: pink, red, white, purple; showy in spring, summer
Light requirement: full sun to part shade
Soil pH tolerance: acid to alkaline
Soil moisture: tolerates moderate drought and poor drainage
Salt tolerance: low
Notes: cultivars available in variety of flower colors; often cut back each spring

Botanical name: *Buxus microphylla*
Common name: Boxwood, Littleleaf Box
Hardiness zones: 6A-10A
Uses: bonsai; edging; foundation; hedge
Florida native: no
Plant type: evergreen shrub
Mature size: 2-5 feet tall by 2-4 feet wide
Flower: inconspicuous
Light requirement: full sun to part shade
Soil pH tolerance: acid to slightly alkaline
Soil moisture: tolerates moderate drought
Salt tolerance: none
Notes: fabulous hedge for small garden spaces

Botanical name: *Caesalpinia pulcherrima*
Common name: Dwarf Poinciana, Barbados Flowerfence
Hardiness zones: 9B-11
Uses: accent, shrub border
Florida native: no
Plant type: evergreen shrub
Mature size: 8-12 feet tall and wide
Flower: orange and yellow; showy year-round
Light requirement: full sun to part shade
Soil pH tolerance: acid to alkaline
Soil moisture: tolerates drought
Salt tolerance: moderate
Notes: striking flowers displayed periodically throughout the year; stems have sharp thorns

Botanical name: *Calliandra haematocephala*
Common name: Powderpuff
Hardiness zones: 9B-11
Uses: hedge; accent; container or planter; small tree
Florida native: no
Plant type: evergreen shrub or tree
Mature size: 12-15 feet tall and wide
Flower: red and pink; showy year-round
Light requirement: full sun to part shade
Soil pH tolerance: acid to slightly alkaline
Soil moisture: tolerates drought
Salt tolerance: low
Notes: puffy flowers cover plant year-round; can be clipped to keep smaller

Botanical name: *Calliandra haematocephala* 'Nana'
Common name: Dwarf Red Powderpuff
Hardiness zones: 9A-11
Uses: hedge; border; container or planter; foundation; attracts butterflies; mass planting
Florida native: no
Plant type: evergreen shrub
Mature size: 3-5 feet tall and wide
Flower: pinkish red; showy year-round
Light requirement: full sun to part shade
Soil pH tolerance: acid to slightly alkaline
Soil moisture: tolerates drought
Salt tolerance: low
Notes: nice for foundations and hedges; this cultivar is much more useful than the species

Botanical name: *Callicarpa americana*
Common name: American Beautyberry
Hardiness zones: 7A-11
Uses: accent; foundation; border; mass
  planting; container or planter; naturalizing
Florida native: yes
Plant type: deciduous shrub
Mature size: 3-8 feet tall and wide
Flower: inconspicuous in spring
Light requirement: full sun to part shade
Soil pH tolerance: acid to slightly alkaline
Soil moisture: tolerates moderate drought
Salt tolerance: low
Notes: bright purple clusters of berries weigh
branches down in fall and winter

Botanical name: *Callistemon citrinus*
Common name: Red Bottlebrush, Lemon
  Bottlebrush
Hardiness zones: 9A-11
Uses: hedge; accent; container or planter
Florida native: no
Plant type: evergreen shrub
Mature size: 10-15 feet tall and wide
Flower: red and very showy in spring, summer
Light requirement: full sun
Soil pH tolerance: acid to slightly alkaline
Soil moisture: tolerates drought
Salt tolerance: moderate
Notes: erect red flowers cover plant all summer;
can be trained into a small tree

Botanical name: *Calycanthus floridus*
Common name: Sweetshrub, Carolina Allspice
Hardiness zones: 5B-10A
Uses: border; screen; espalier; accent
Florida native: yes
Plant type: deciduous shrub
Mature size: 6-9 feet tall by 6-12 feet wide
Flower: maroon; showy in spring, summer
Light requirement: full sun to full shade
Soil pH tolerance: acid to slightly alkaline
Soil moisture: tolerates moderate drought and
  poor drainage
Salt tolerance: low
Notes: highly fragrant flowers partially hidden
by dense foliage

Botanical name: *Calyptranthes pallens*
Common name: Spicewood, Pale Lidflower
Hardiness zones: 10B-11
Uses: screen; border; espalier; hedge
Florida native: yes
Plant type: evergreen shrub or small tree
Mature size: 10-15 feet tall by 6-10 feet wide
Flower: inconspicuous
Light requirement: full sun to part shade
Soil pH tolerance: acid to slightly alkaline
Soil moisture: tolerates moderate drought and
    poor drainage
Salt tolerance: moderate
Notes: tall, narrow plant makes great screen

Botanical name: *Camellia japonica*
Common name: Camellia
Hardiness zones: 7A-9B
Uses: screen; accent; container or planter;
    foundation; small tree
Florida native: no
Plant type: evergreen shrub or tree
Mature size: 7-12 feet tall by 5-10 feet wide
Flower: pink, red and white; showy in winter
    and spring
Light requirement: part sun to part shade
Soil pH tolerance: acid
Soil moisture: tolerates moderate drought
Salt tolerance: low
Notes: Sasanqua Camellia (*C. sasanqua*) flowers
in fall and winter; grows slowly

Botanical name: *Canella winterana*
Common name: Winter Cinnamon, Wild
    Cinnamon
Hardiness zones: 10B-11
Uses: hedge; espalier; screen
Florida native: yes
Plant type: evergreen shrub or small tree
Mature size: 20-30 feet tall by 6-8 feet wide
Flower: showy white in summer, fall
Light requirement: full sun to part shade
Soil pH tolerance: acid to alkaline
Soil moisture: tolerates drought
Salt tolerance: high
Notes: showy red fruit in fall and winter
contrasts nicely with dark green foliage

Botanical name: *Capparis cynophallophora*
Common name: Jamaican Caper
Hardiness zones: 10A-11
Uses: screen; attracts butterflies
Florida native: yes
Plant type: evergreen shrub
Mature size: 6-15 feet tall and wide
Flower: white and pink; showy in spring
Light requirement: full sun to part shade
Soil pH tolerance: acid to slightly alkaline
Soil moisture: tolerates drought
Salt tolerance: high
Notes: delicate flowers borne throughout the plant

Botanical name: *Carissa macrocarpa*
Common name: Dwarf Natal-Plum
Hardiness zones: 9B-11
Uses: dune stabilization; bonsai; mass planting; container or planter; ground cover
Florida native: no
Plant type: low evergreen shrub or tall ground cover
Mature size: 1-2 feet tall by 4-8 feet wide
Flower: white; showy in summer
Light requirement: full sun to part shade
Soil pH tolerance: acid to alkaline
Soil moisture: tolerates drought
Salt tolerance: high
Notes: bright red fruits are showy and edible

Botanical name: *Casasia clusiifolia*
Common name: Seven-Year Apple
Hardiness zones: 10B-11
Uses: container or planter; hedge; screen; accent
Florida native: yes
Plant type: evergreen shrub
Mature size: 8-20 feet tall and wide
Flower: showy periodically throughout the year
Light requirement: full sun to part shade
Soil pH tolerance: acid to alkaline
Soil moisture: tolerates drought
Salt tolerance: high
Notes: large foliage lends coarse texture to landscape

Botanical name: *Cassia alata*
Common name: Candle-Bush
Hardiness zones: 10A-11
Uses: accent; container or planter; mass
  planting
Florida native: no
Plant type: deciduous shrub
Mature size: 5-10 feet tall and wide
Flower: yellow; showy in summer, fall
Light requirement: full sun
Soil pH tolerance: acid to slightly alkaline
Soil moisture: tolerates moderate drought
Salt tolerance: unknown
Notes: bright yellow flowers are held well above
light green foliage; often cut back to keep small

Botanical name: *Cassia bicapsularis*
  (= *Senna pendula*)
Common name: Cassia
Hardiness zones: 8B-11
Uses: accent; container or planter
Florida native: no   **INVASIVE**
Plant type: deciduous shrub
Mature size: 6-8 feet tall and wide
Flower: yellow; showy in fall
Light requirement: full sun to part shade
Soil pH tolerance: acid to slightly alkaline
Soil moisture: tolerates moderate drought
Salt tolerance: moderate
Notes: bright yellow flowers fill canopy; most
plants require stakes to hold them erect;
escaped from cultivation in several south
Florida counties

Botanical name: *Chamaedorea microspadix*
Common name: Microspadix Palm, Hardy
  Bamboo Palm
Hardiness zones: 8B-11
Uses: container or planter; screen; accent; mass
  planting; indoors
Florida native: no **Plant type:** clumping palm
Mature size: 6-10 feet tall by 5-8 feet wide
Flower: yellow; showy periodically throughout
  the year
Light requirement: part shade to full shade
Soil pH tolerance: acid to slightly alkaline
Soil moisture: drought sensitive
Salt tolerance: low
Notes: wonderful accent; provide regular
fertilizer to maintain foliage color; remove dead
lower leaves, remove flowers as they emerge to
maintain vigorous stems

Botanical name: *Chamaerops humilis*
Common name: European Fan Palm
Hardiness zones: 8B-11
Uses: container or planter; accent; indoors
Florida native: no
Plant type: palm
Mature size: 10-15 feet tall by 6-10 feet wide
Flower: inconspicuous
Light requirement: full sun to part shade
Soil pH tolerance: acid to alkaline
Soil moisture: tolerates drought
Salt tolerance: high
Notes: foliage is bluish green on some plants; sharp spines on petiole

Botanical name: *Chrysobalanus icaco*
Common name: Cocoplum
Hardiness zones: 10B-11
Uses: foundation; hedge; small tree
Florida native: yes
Plant type: evergreen shrub or tree
Mature size: 10-20 feet tall by 10-15 feet wide
Flower: inconspicuous in spring
Light requirement: full sun to part shade
Soil pH tolerance: acid to alkaline
Soil moisture: tolerates drought
Salt tolerance: high
Notes: new foliage emerges red; dwarf variety grows to about 3 feet tall

Botanical name: *Citharexylum fruticosum*
Common name: Fiddlewood
Hardiness zones: 10B-11
Uses: container or planter; espalier; border; small tree
Florida native: yes
Plant type: evergreen shrub or small tree
Mature size: 15-25 feet tall by 8-15 feet wide
Flower: white; showy periodically during the year
Light requirement: full sun to part shade
Soil pH tolerance: acid to alkaline
Soil moisture: tolerates drought
Salt tolerance: moderate
Notes: fast growth makes it best suited as small tree; shiny green foliage

Botanical name: *Codiaeum variegatum*
Common name: Croton
Hardiness zones: 10B-11
Uses: hedge; mass planting; container or planter; indoors; accent; attracts butterflies
Florida native: no
Plant type: evergreen shrub
Mature size: 3-8 feet tall by 3-6 feet wide
Flower: inconspicuous
Light requirement: full sun to part shade
Soil pH tolerance: acid to alkaline
Soil moisture: tolerates drought
Salt tolerance: moderate
Notes: variegated foliage with striking red, orange, and yellow markings

Botanical name: *Conocarpus erectus* var. seriacus
Common name: Buttonwood
Hardiness zones: 10B-11
Uses: accent; screen; hedge; bonsai; small tree
Florida native: yes
Plant type: large, evergreen shrub or tree
Mature size: 15-20 feet tall by 20-30 feet wide
Flower: inconspicuous
Light requirement: full sun
Soil pH tolerance: acid to alkaline
Soil moisture: tolerates drought and poor drainage
Salt tolerance: very high
Notes: silver foliage makes this a popular hedge

Botanical name: *Cordyline terminalis*
Common name: Ti Plant
Hardiness zones: 10B-11
Uses: perennial border; accent; container or planter; indoors; mass planting
Florida native: no
Plant type: erect, evergreen shrub
Mature size: 3-10 feet tall by 2-4 feet wide
Flower: inconspicuous
Light requirement: full sun to part shade
Soil pH tolerance: acid to slightly alkaline
Soil moisture: tolerates moderate drought
Salt tolerance: none
Notes: foliage brightly striped with red, pink, and black

Botanical name: *Cortaderia selloana*
Common name: Pampas Grass
Hardiness zones: 5B-11
Uses: screen; mass planting; accent; cut flowers
Florida native: no
Plant type: ornamental grass; perennial
Mature size: 8-10 feet tall and wide
Flower: creamy white; showy in summer, fall
Light requirement: full sun to part shade
Soil pH tolerance: acid to alkaline
Soil moisture: tolerates drought
Salt tolerance: moderate
Notes: leaves have sharp edges that cut fingers; too large for many Florida residences; use native gamma grasses instead

Botanical name: *Crinum americanum*
Common name: String-Lily, Swamp-Lily
Hardiness zones: 7A-11
Uses: perennial border; mass planting; accent
Florida native: yes
Plant type: tuber; perennial
Mature size: 1-2 feet tall and wide
Flower: white; showy year-round
Light requirement: full sun to part shade
Soil pH tolerance: acid to slightly alkaline
Soil moisture: tolerates moderate drought and poor drainage; grows in and near water
Salt tolerance: moderate
Notes: lends fabulous texture to garden in wet spot

Botanical name: *Crinum* x *amabile*
Common name: Giant Spider-Lily
Hardiness zones: 8B-11
Uses: perennial border; mass planting; accent
Florida native: no
Plant type: tuber; perennial
Mature size: 3-5 feet tall and wide
Flower: maroon, pink and white; showy year-round
Light requirement: full sun to part shade
Soil pH tolerance: acid to slightly alkaline
Soil moisture: tolerates moderate drought and poor drainage
Salt tolerance: moderate
Notes: large accent plant that looks great when surrounded by low ground cover

Botanical name: *Cuphea hyssopifolia*
Common name: False Heather, Mexican Heather
Hardiness zones: 8B-11
Uses: ground cover; edging; tiny hedge; perennial border; mass planting; container
Florida native: no
Plant type: woody perennial
Mature size: 1-2 feet tall by 2-3 feet wide
Flower: lavender or white; showy year-round
Light requirement: full sun to part shade
Soil pH tolerance: acid to alkaline
Soil moisture: tolerates moderate drought
Salt tolerance: low
Notes: often reseeds itself; attracts butterflies

Botanical name: *Cuphea ignea*
Common name: Cigar Plant, Cigar Flower
Hardiness zones: 9B-11
Uses: perennial border; container or planter; accent; attracts hummingbirds
Florida native: no
Plant type: shrubby perennial
Mature size: 2-3 feet tall and wide
Flower: reddish orange; showy year-round
Light requirement: full sun to part shade
Soil pH tolerance: acid to alkaline
Soil moisture: tolerates moderate drought
Salt tolerance: low
Notes: fabulous for perennial border

Botanical name: *Cycas circinalis*
Common name: Queen Sago
Hardiness zones: 10A-11
Uses: accent
Florida native: no
Plant type: evergreen shrub
Mature size: 6-15 feet tall by 8-12 feet wide
Flower: inflorescence is borne in the center of the leaf mass
Light requirement: full sun to part shade
Soil pH tolerance: acid to slightly alkaline
Soil moisture: tolerates drought
Salt tolerance: moderate
Notes: best suited for large landscapes due to its size; watch for scale infestation

Botanical name: *Cycas revoluta*
Common name: King Sago
Hardiness zones: 8B-11
Uses: container or planter; mass planting; accent; indoors
Florida native: no **Plant type:** evergreen shrub
Mature size: 3-10 feet tall by 6 feet wide
Flower: inflorescence is borne in the center of the leaf mass
Light requirement: full sun to part shade
Soil pH tolerance: acid to slightly alkaline
Soil moisture: tolerates drought
Salt tolerance: high
Notes: grows slowly; sharp leaves; watch for scale and mealybug infestation; regular manganese applications help prevent distorted yellow leaves

Botanical name: *Cyperus alternifolius*
Common name: Umbrella Sedge
Hardiness zones: 8B-11
Uses: mass planting; container or planter; water garden **Florida native:** no
Plant type: herbaceous perennial
Mature size: 4-8 feet tall
Flower: green; showy year-round
Light requirement: full sun to part shade
Soil pH tolerance: acid to slightly alkaline
Soil moisture: drought sensitive; tolerates poor drainage
Salt tolerance: low
Notes: unique, upright plant; best used in moist location or in water; freezing temperatures brown leaves and flowers; plants spread by underground rhizomes, could become invasive

Botanical name: *Cyrtomium falcatum*
Common name: Holly Fern, Japanese Holly Fern
Hardiness zones: 8A-11
Uses: mass planting; ground cover; edging; indoors
Florida native: no
Plant type: evergreen, herbaceous ground cover
Mature size: 2-3 feet tall by 2-4 feet wide
Flower: spores are borne under leaflets
Light requirement: part shade to full shade
Soil pH tolerance: acid
Soil moisture: drought sensitive
Salt tolerance: none
Notes: water during drought and fertilize twice each year

Botanical name: *Dieffenbachia* spp.
Common name: Giant Dumbcane
Hardiness zones: 10B-11
Uses: perennial border; container or planter; accent; indoors
Florida native: no
Plant type: evergreen, herbaceous perennial
Mature size: 4-7 feet tall by 2-3 feet wide
Flower: inconspicuous
Light requirement: part shade to full shade
Soil pH tolerance: acid
Soil moisture: provide well-drained soil; drought sensitive
Salt tolerance: low
Notes: large foliage lends coarse texture to landscape

Botanical name: *Dietes vegeta*
Common name: African Iris, Butterfly Iris
Hardiness zones: 8B-11
Uses: perennial border; mass planting; water garden; accent **Florida native:** no
Plant type: evergreen, herbaceous perennial
Mature size: 2-6 feet tall by 2-3 feet wide
Flower: white; showy periodically throughout the year
Light requirement: full sun to part shade
Soil pH tolerance: acid to slightly alkaline
Soil moisture: tolerates moderate drought and poor drainage
Salt tolerance: none
Notes: provide regular water during drought for best growth; subfreezing temperatures turn foliage brown

Botanical name: *Dodonaea viscosa*
Common name: Varnish-Leaf
Hardiness zones: 9A-11
Uses: hedge; accent; espalier; screen
Florida native: yes
Plant type: evergreen shrub
Mature size: 10-15 feet tall by 6-15 feet wide
Flower: inconspicuous
Light requirement: full sun
Soil pH tolerance: acid to alkaline
Soil moisture: tolerates drought
Salt tolerance: high
Notes: fine-textured foliage makes this a good candidate for hedge

Botanical name: *Dombeya* spp.
Common name: Tropical Snowball
Hardiness zones: 9A-11
Uses: container or planter; accent; cut flowers; screen
Florida native: no
Plant type: evergreen shrub
Mature size: 6-10 feet tall and wide
Flower: pink; showy in summer, fall
Light requirement: full sun
Soil pH tolerance: acid to alkaline
Soil moisture: drought sensitive
Salt tolerance: none
Notes: large, wonderful flower makes this plant popular among gardeners

Botanical name: *Dracaena deremensis*
Common name: Dracaena
Hardiness zones: 10B-11
Uses: mass planting; container or planter; perennial border; indoors; accent
Florida native: no
Plant type: evergreen shrub
Mature size: 8-12 feet tall by 3-5 feet wide
Flower: inconspicuous
Light requirement: part to full shade
Soil pH tolerance: acid to slightly alkaline
Soil moisture: tolerates moderate drought and poor drainage
Salt tolerance: none
Notes: great house plant or garden accent

Botanical name: *Dracaena marginata*
Common name: Red-Edged Dracaena, Madagascar Dragon-Tree
Hardiness zones: 10B-11
Uses: container or planter; perennial border; indoors; accent
Florida native: no
Plant type: evergreen shrub
Mature size: 8-12 feet tall by 3-8 feet wide
Flower: inconspicuous
Light requirement: full sun to part shade
Soil pH tolerance: acid to slightly alkaline
Soil moisture: tolerates drought
Salt tolerance: none
Notes: cut stems back occasionally to force growth at bottom and to keep plant full

Botanical name: *Duranta repens*
Common name: Golden Dewdrop
Hardiness zones: 9A-11
Uses: hedge; mass planting; container or planter; screen; espalier; attracts butterflies
Florida native: possibly
Plant type: sprawling evergreen shrub
Mature size: 8-15 feet tall and wide
Flower: purple or white; showy in spring, summer, fall
Light requirement: full sun to part shade
Soil pH tolerance: acid to slightly alkaline
Soil moisture: tolerates drought
Salt tolerance: moderate
Notes: showy yellow fruit fills canopy; fruit poisonous to humans but consumed by birds; frost kills plants to the ground

Botanical name: *Elaeagnus pungens*
Common name: Silverthorn, Thorny Elaeagnus
Hardiness zones: 7A-10B
Uses: bank stabilization; screen; espalier
Florida native: no
Plant type: evergreen shrub
Mature size: 10-20 feet tall and wide
Flower: white; fragrant in spring and winter
Light requirement: full sun to part shade
Soil pH tolerance: acid to alkaline
Soil moisture: tolerates drought and poor drainage
Salt tolerance: high
Notes: large, grows fast, not suited for most residences or any other locations; thorns can inflict pain

Botanical name: *Eugenia foetida*
Common name: Spanish Stopper, Box-Leaf Eugenia
Hardiness zones: 10A-11
Uses: container or planter; hedge; screen
Florida native: yes
Plant type: evergreen shrub
Mature size: 12-20 feet tall by 8-15 feet wide
Flower: white; inconspicuous
Light requirement: full sun to part shade
Soil pH tolerance: acid to alkaline
Soil moisture: tolerates drought
Salt tolerance: high
Notes: great hedge

Botanical name: *Eugenia rhombea*
Common name: Red Stopper, Spiceberry
Hardiness zones: 10B-11
Uses: container or planter; hedge; screen; small
    tree
Florida native: yes
Plant type: evergreen shrub or tree
Mature size: 15-20 feet tall by 10-15 feet wide
Flower: white; somewhat showy in summer
Light requirement: full sun to part shade
Soil pH tolerance: acid to alkaline
Soil moisture: tolerates drought
Salt tolerance: high
Notes: delicate flowers contrast nicely against
olive-green foliage

Botanical name: *Eugenia uniflora*
Common name: Surinam Cherry
Hardiness zones: 9B-11
Uses: screen; hedge; container or planter; small
    tree (plant can invade native woodlands)
Florida native: no   **INVASIVE**
Plant type: evergreen shrub or tree
Mature size: 8-20 feet tall by 6-15 feet wide
Flower: showy in spring
Light requirement: full sun to part shade
Soil pH tolerance: acid to alkaline
Soil moisture: tolerates moderate drought
Salt tolerance: moderate
Notes: common plant with edible fruit and red
new foliage; occasionally trained into tree; seeds
germinate readily in nearby landscapes and can
become invasive

Botanical name: *Fatsia japonica*
Common name: Fatsia
Hardiness zones: 8A-11
Uses: border; mass planting; container or
    planter; indoors; accent
Florida native: no
Plant type: evergreen shrub
Mature size: 5-8 feet tall by 3-10 feet wide
Flower: white; showy in fall
Light requirement: part shade to full shade
Soil pH tolerance: acid to slightly alkaline
Soil moisture: tolerates moderate drought
Salt tolerance: low
Notes: fabulous coarse-textured accent for
shaded location

Botanical name: *Feijoa sellowiana*
Common name: Pineapple Guava
Hardiness zones: 8A-11
Uses: accent; screen; hedge; fruit; small tree
Florida native: no
Plant type: evergreen shrub or tree
Mature size: 10-15 feet tall and wide
Flower: red and pink; showy in spring
Light requirement: full sun to part shade
Soil pH tolerance: acid to slightly alkaline
Soil moisture: tolerates drought
Salt tolerance: high
Notes: though used most as hedge, displays wonderful bark when grown as tree; flowers are beautiful

Botanical name: *Ficus benjamina*
Common name: Weeping Fig
Hardiness zones: 10B-11
Uses: container or planter; hedge; house plant
Florida native: no   **Plant type:** tree
Mature size: 45-60 feet tall by 60-100 feet wide
Flower: inconspicuous
Light requirement: full sun to shade
Soil pH tolerance: acid to alkaline
Soil moisture: tolerates drought and poor drainage
Salt tolerance: moderate
Notes: foliage remains dense when clipped into hedge; invades nearby landscapes; roots are destructive

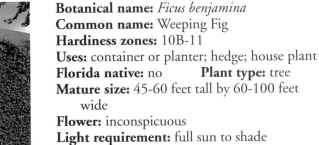

Botanical name: *Forestiera segregata*
Common name: Florida Privet
Hardiness zones: 8B-11
Uses: container or planter; hedge; espalier; screen; attracts butterflies
Florida native: yes
Plant type: evergreen shrub
Mature size: 10-15 feet tall by 5-10 feet wide
Flower: white; inconspicuous in spring and winter
Light requirement: full sun to part shade
Soil pH tolerance: acid to alkaline
Soil moisture: tolerates drought and poor drainage
Salt tolerance: high
Notes: small foliage makes this a great candidate for hedge or screen

Botanical name: *Fothergilla gardenii*
Common name: Dwarf Fothergilla
Hardiness zones: 5A-8A
Uses: hedge; accent; border; mass planting
Florida native: yes
Plant type: deciduous shrub
Mature size: 4-6 feet tall and wide
Flower: white; showy in spring
Light requirement: full sun to part shade
Soil pH tolerance: acid
Soil moisture: tolerates moderate drought and
    poor drainage
Salt tolerance: unknown
Notes: red fall foliage adds interest to autumn
landscape

Botanical name: *Galphimia glauca*
Common name: Thryallis, Shower-of-Gold
Hardiness zones: 9B-11
Uses: hedge; perennial border; mass planting;
    container or planter
Florida native: no
Plant type: evergreen shrub
Mature size: 5-9 feet tall by 4-6 feet wide
Flower: yellow; showy year-round
Light requirement: full sun
Soil pH tolerance: acid to slightly alkaline
Soil moisture: tolerates moderate drought
Salt tolerance: low
Notes: filled with bright yellow flowers nearly
year-round

Botanical name: *Gamolepis chrysanthemoides*
Common name: African Bush-Daisy,
    Daisy-Bush
Hardiness zones: 8B-11
Uses: mass planting; perennial border;
    container or planter; attracts butterflies
Florida native: no
Plant type: herbaceous perennial
Mature size: 2-3 feet tall and wide
Flower: yellow; showy in warm weather
Light requirement: full sun
Soil pH tolerance: acid to slightly alkaline
Soil moisture: tolerates moderate drought
Salt tolerance: none
Notes: full sun essential for best flowering;
tends to fall over as it grows taller

Botanical name: *Gardenia jasminoides*
Common name: Gardenia, Cape-Jasmine
Hardiness zones: 8A-10B
Uses: bonsai; screen; hedge; border; container or planter; cut flowers
Florida native: no
Plant type: evergreen shrub
Mature size: 4-8 feet tall and wide
Flower: white; fragrant and showy in spring
Light requirement: full sun to full shade
Soil pH tolerance: acid to slightly alkaline
Soil moisture: tolerates moderate drought
Salt tolerance: none
Notes: scale insects and whiteflies can be troublesome; cultivars available for flower and plant size

Botanical name: *Graptophyllum pictum*
Common name: Caricature Plant
Hardiness zones: 10B-11
Uses: container or planter; foundation; border; accent; mass planting
Florida native: no
Plant type: shrub; perennial
Mature size: 3-8 feet tall by 2-5 feet wide
Flower: showy pink in summer
Light requirement: full sun to full shade
Soil pH tolerance: acid to slightly alkaline
Soil moisture: drought sensitive; tolerates poor drainage
Salt tolerance: none
Notes: tender plant with variegated foliage; suited for shaded location

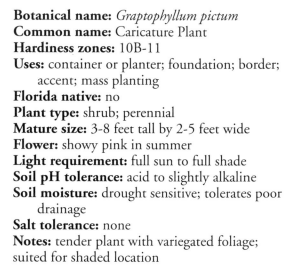

Botanical name: *Guaiacum* spp.
Common name: Lignum Vitae
Hardiness zones: 10B-11
Uses: container or planter; accent; bonsai; small tree
Florida native: yes
Plant type: evergreen shrub or tree
Mature size: 8-12 feet tall by 8-12 feet wide
Flower: showy year-round
Light requirement: full sun to part shade
Soil pH tolerance: acid to alkaline
Soil moisture: tolerates drought and poor drainage
Salt tolerance: high
Notes: *G. officinale* is native to the Keys; showy bark shows nicely with lower branches removed

Botanical name: *Hamelia patens*
Common name: Firebush
Hardiness zones: 9A-11
Uses: hedge; accent; screen; perennial border; mass planting; attracts butterflies and hummingbirds
Florida native: yes
Plant type: evergreen shrub
Mature size: 6-12 feet tall by 5-8 feet wide
Flower: reddish orange; showy year-round
Light requirement: full sun to full shade
Soil pH tolerance: acid to alkaline
Soil moisture: tolerates moderate drought and poor drainage
Salt tolerance: none
Notes: plants killed to ground by freezing temperatures re-emerge in spring

Botanical name: *Hedychium coronarium*
Common name: Butterfly Ginger
Hardiness zones: 8B-11
Uses: accent; border; mass planting; indoors
Florida native: no
Plant type: herbaceous perennial
Mature size: 4-5 feet tall by 2-6 feet wide
Flower: white; fragrant and showy in summer and fall
Light requirement: full sun to part shade
Soil pH tolerance: acid to slightly alkaline
Soil moisture: tolerates moderate drought and poor drainage
Salt tolerance: moderate
Notes: tender plant that adds coarse texture to landscape, especially planted en masse

Botanical name: *Heliconia* spp.
Common name: Heliconia
Hardiness zones: 10B-11
Uses: accent; cut flowers; indoors
Florida native: no
Plant type: herbaceous perennial
Mature size: 2-15 feet tall by 3-6 feet wide
Flower: orange, red, yellow; showy in spring, summer
Light requirement: full sun to part shade
Soil pH tolerance: acid to alkaline
Soil moisture: tolerates moderate drought
Salt tolerance: moderate
Notes: plant size and flower color vary depending on species

Botanical name: *Hibiscus rosa-sinensis*
Common name: Tropical Hibiscus, Chinese Hibiscus
Hardiness zones: 9A-11
Uses: screen; hedge; accent; container or planter; attracts butterflies and humming-birds
Florida native: no
Plant type: evergreen shrub
Mature size: 7-15 feet tall by 6-10 feet wide
Flower: red, pink, lavender; showy year-round
Light requirement: full sun to part shade
Soil pH tolerance: acid to slightly alkaline
Soil moisture: tolerates moderate drought
Salt tolerance: very high
Notes: tough plant that keeps flowering in full sun

Botanical name: *Hibiscus syriacus*
Common name: Rose-of-Sharon, Shrub-Althea
Hardiness zones: 5B-9A
Uses: accent; container or planter
Florida native: no
Plant type: deciduous shrub, small tree
Mature size: 8-12 feet tall by 4-10 feet wide
Flower: red, pink, lavender; showy in summer
Light requirement: full sun to part shade
Soil pH tolerance: acid
Soil moisture: tolerates moderate drought
Salt tolerance: moderate
Notes: upright habit and showy flowers make this nice accent for sunny location

Botanical name: *Holmskioldia sanguinea*
Common name: Chinese Hat Plant
Hardiness zones: 10B-11
Uses: container or planter; hedge; accent; border
Florida native: no
Plant type: evergreen shrub
Mature size: 5-8 feet tall and wide
Flower: orange; showy year-round
Light requirement: full sun to part shade
Soil pH tolerance: acid to slightly alkaline
Soil moisture: tolerates moderate drought
Salt tolerance: moderate
Notes: striking flower makes this ideal for prominent spot in landscape

Botanical name: *Hydrangea macrophylla*
Common name: Garden Hydrangea
Hardiness zones: 5B-9A
Uses: border; mass planting; foundation; accent; cut flowers
Florida native: no
Plant type: deciduous shrub
Mature size: 3-6 feet tall and wide
Flower: blue, pink; showy in spring, summer
Light requirement: part shade to full shade
Soil pH tolerance: acid to slightly alkaline
Soil moisture: drought sensitive; tolerates poor drainage
Salt tolerance: none
Notes: wonderful garden plant that flowers for up to six months; many cultivars available

Botanical name: *Hydrangea quercifolia*
Common name: Oak-Leaf Hydrangea
Hardiness zones: 5B-9B
Uses: border; mass planting; accent; screen
Florida native: yes
Plant type: deciduous shrub
Mature size: 8-10 feet tall and wide
Flower: white; showy in spring
Light requirement: mostly sunny to part shade
Soil pH tolerance: acid to slightly alkaline
Soil moisture: tolerates moderate drought and poor drainage
Salt tolerance: low
Notes: great accent due to large leaves; choose dwarf cultivar for small landscapes; plants are expensive because they are challenging to propagate

Botanical name: *Ilex cornuta* 'Burfordii Nana'
Common name: Compact Burford Holly, Dwarf Burford Holly
Hardiness zones: 7A-9B
Uses: bonsai; foundation; hedge; screen; cut foliage/twigs
Florida native: no
Plant type: evergreen shrub
Mature size: 10-15 feet tall and wide
Flower: white; inconspicuous; attracts bees
Light requirement: full sun to part shade
Soil pH tolerance: acid to slightly alkaline
Soil moisture: tolerates drought
Salt tolerance: moderate
Notes: watch for scale insects; foliage has sharp spine at tip

Botanical name: *Ilex cornuta 'Rotunda'*
Common name: Dwarf Chinese Holly
Hardiness zones: 7A-9B
Uses: foundation; border; mass planting; cut foliage/twigs
Florida native: no
Plant type: evergreen shrub
Mature size: 4-6 feet tall and wide
Flower: inconspicuous
Light requirement: full sun to part shade
Soil pH tolerance: acid to slightly alkaline
Soil moisture: tolerates drought
Salt tolerance: moderate
Notes: suited for residential landscapes because it is easy to maintain at a small size; foliage edged with sharp spines

Botanical name: *Ilex crenata*
Common name: Japanese Holly
Hardiness zones: 6A-9A
Uses: foundation; mass planting; hedge
Florida native: no
Plant type: evergreen shrub
Mature size: 6-10 feet tall by 5-8 feet wide
Flower: inconspicuous
Light requirement: full sun to part shade
Soil pH tolerance: acid to slightly alkaline
Soil moisture: tolerates drought
Salt tolerance: moderate
Notes: suited for residential landscapes because it is easy to maintain at a small size; many cultivars available for size and shape of canopy

Botanical name: *Ilex glabra*
Common name: Gallberry, Inkberry
Hardiness zones: 5A-10A
Uses: accent; screen; foundation; mass planting
Florida native: yes
Plant type: deciduous shrub
Mature size: 6-8 feet tall and wide
Flower: inconspicuous
Light requirement: full sun to part shade
Soil pH tolerance: acid to slightly alkaline
Soil moisture: tolerates moderate drought and poor drainage
Salt tolerance: moderate
Notes: yellow fall color in northern Florida

Botanical name: *Ilex vomitoria*
Common name: Dwarf Yaupon Holly
Hardiness zones: 7A-10B
Uses: dune stabilization; bonsai; foundation;
    mass planting; hedge
Florida native: yes
Plant type: evergreen shrub
Mature size: 4-7 feet tall by 6-10 feet wide
Flower: inconspicuous
Light requirement: full sun to part shade
Soil pH tolerance: acid to slightly alkaline
Soil moisture: tolerates drought and poor
    drainage
Salt tolerance: high
Notes: new foliage is red; stays dense but
requires yearly clipping to keep within bounds

Botanical name: *Illicium floridanum*
Common name: Florida Anise, Purple Anise
Hardiness zones: 8A-10B
Uses: hedge; espalier; screen; accent
Florida native: yes
Plant type: evergreen shrub
Mature size: 10-15 feet tall by 10 feet wide
Flower: red; slightly fragrant and showy in
    spring
Light requirement: full sun to part shade
Soil pH tolerance: acid to slightly alkaline
Soil moisture: tolerates some drought
Salt tolerance: low
Notes: maroon-red flowers cover plant for two
weeks each year

Botanical name: *Illicium parviflorum*
Common name: Anise, Small Anise
Hardiness zones: 7B-10A
Uses: hedge; espalier; screen; small tree
Florida native: yes
Plant type: evergreen shrub or tree
Mature size: 15-20 feet tall by 10-15 feet wide
Flower: yellow; mostly inconspicuous in
    summer
Light requirement: full sun to mostly shaded
Soil pH tolerance: acid to slightly alkaline
Soil moisture: tolerates drought
Salt tolerance: low
Notes: fabulous screen; responds well to
clipping

Botanical name: *Ixora coccinea*
Common name: Ixora
Hardiness zones: 10A-11
Uses: foundation; screen; container or planter; hedge; accent; attracts hummingbirds
Florida native: no
Plant type: evergreen shrub
Mature size: 10-15 feet tall by 6-10 feet wide
Flower: red and yellow; showy year-round
Light requirement: full sun to part shade
Soil pH tolerance: acid to slightly alkaline
Soil moisture: tolerates moderate drought
Salt tolerance: low
Notes: fertilize regularly; smaller cultivars and related species available in variety of flower colors; chlorosis develops without regular manganese applications in alkaline soil

Botanical name: *Jasminum multiflorum*
Common name: Downy Jasmine
Hardiness zones: 9B-11
Uses: foundation; mass planting; border; hedge; cascades down a wall
Florida native: no
Plant type: viny, evergreen shrub
Mature size: 6-10 feet tall by 4-10 feet wide
Flower: white; showy in summer and fall
Light requirement: full sun to part shade
Soil pH tolerance: acid to alkaline
Soil moisture: tolerates moderate drought
Salt tolerance: none
Notes: shiny foliage and bright white flowers combine to make nice accent

Botanical name: *Jatropha integerrima*
Common name: Peregrina
Hardiness zones: 10B-11
Uses: accent; container or planter; attracts hummingbirds and butterflies
Florida native: no
Plant type: evergreen shrub
Mature size: 10-15 feet tall and wide
Flower: red; showy year-round
Light requirement: full sun to part shade
Soil pH tolerance: acid to alkaline
Soil moisture: tolerates moderate drought
Salt tolerance: moderate
Notes: can be trained into an attractive small tree

Botanical name: *Juniperus chinensis*
    'Blue Vase'
Common name: 'Blue Vase' Juniper
Hardiness zones: 7B-10B
Uses: screen; border; mass planting; accent
Florida native: no
Plant type: evergreen shrub
Mature size: 8-12 feet tall by 6-8 feet wide
Flower: inconspicuous
Light requirement: full sun
Soil pH tolerance: acid to alkaline
Soil moisture: tolerates drought
Salt tolerance: moderate
Notes: blue foliage makes this a popular choice
as an accent plant

Botanical name: *Juniperus chinensis* 'Torulosa'
Common name: 'Torulosa' Juniper
Hardiness zones: 5B-11
Uses: accent; screen; container or planter;
    espalier
Florida native: no
Plant type: evergreen shrub
Mature size: 10-15 feet tall by 6-8 feet wide
Flower: inconspicuous
Light requirement: full sun
Soil pH tolerance: acid to alkaline
Soil moisture: tolerates drought
Salt tolerance: high
Notes: bright green accent for a sunny location

Botanical name: *Justicia brandegeana*
Common name: Shrimp Plant
Hardiness zones: 8B-11
Uses: perennial border; mass planting;
    container or planter; attracts humming-
    birds
Florida native: no
Plant type: herbaceous perennial
Mature size: 3-4 feet tall and wide
Flower: red; showy year-round
Light requirement: full sun to full shade
Soil pH tolerance: acid to slightly alkaline
Soil moisture: tolerates some drought
Salt tolerance: none
Notes: flowers periodically year-round, even in
a partly shaded location; fertilize regularly to
keep foliage green; spreads rapidly

Botanical name: *Justicia carnea*
Common name: Jacobinia, Flamingo Plant
Hardiness zones: 8B-11
Uses: foundation; perennial border; mass planting; container or planter; cut flowers
Florida native: no
Plant type: herbaceous perennial
Mature size: 3-5 feet tall by 2-3 feet wide
Flower: pink or white; showy periodically throughout the year
Light requirement: part sun to full shade
Soil pH tolerance: acid to slightly alkaline
Soil moisture: drought sensitive
Salt tolerance: none
Notes: one of the prettiest flowering perennials for shaded gardens

Botanical name: *Lagerstroemia* spp. and hybrids and cultivars
Common name: Crape Myrtle
Hardiness zones: 7A-9B, 10A
Uses: container or planter; accent; small tree
Florida native: no
Plant type: deciduous ground cover, shrub, tree
Mature size: 3-30 feet tall and wide
Flower: pink, red, lavender, white; showy in spring and summer
Light requirement: full sun
Soil pH tolerance: acid to alkaline
Soil moisture: tolerates drought
Salt tolerance: moderate
Notes: select only disease-resistant hybrids; some cultivars grow poorly south of zone 9A

Botanical name: *Leucophyllum frutescens*
Common name: Texas Sage, Silverleaf
Hardiness zones: 8A-10B
Uses: hedge; mass planting; container or planter; accent
Florida native: no
Plant type: evergreen shrub
Mature size: 5-8 feet tall by 4-6 feet wide
Flower: lavender; showy in spring, summer
Light requirement: full sun
Soil pH tolerance: acid to alkaline
Soil moisture: tolerates drought
Salt tolerance: moderate
Notes: plant in sunny location for best growth and flowering; plants decline in shaded locations

Botanical name: *Leucothoe axillaris*
Common name: Dog-Hobble, Coastal
    Leucothoe
Hardiness zones: 5B-9B
Uses: accent; mass planting; ground cover;
    border
Florida native: yes
Plant type: ground cover
Mature size: 2-6 feet tall by 6-10 feet wide
Flower: inconspicuous in spring
Light requirement: part shade to full shade
Soil pH tolerance: acid
Soil moisture: tolerates moderate drought and
    poor drainage
Salt tolerance: low
Notes: unfortunate name for a showy native
plant

Botanical name: *Ligustrum japonicum*
Common name: Japanese Privet
Hardiness zones: 7B-10A
Uses: screen; accent; hedge; container or
    planter; small tree
Florida native: no
Plant type: evergreen shrub or tree
Mature size: 8-12 feet tall by 15-25 feet wide
Flower: white; showy in spring and summer
Light requirement: full sun to part shade
Soil pH tolerance: acid to slightly alkaline
Soil moisture: tolerates moderate drought
Salt tolerance: high
Notes: nice small tree; when clipping into
hedge, keep top narrower than bottom; could
seed into surrounding landscapes

Botanical name: *Ligustrum sinense*
    'Variegatum'
Common name: Variegated Chinese Privet
Hardiness zones: 7B-10B
Uses: bonsai; hedge; border; mass planting
Florida native: no   **INVASIVE**
Plant type: evergreen shrub
Mature size: 8-15 feet tall by 8-15 feet wide
Flower: white; showy in spring
Light requirement: full sun to part shade
Soil pH tolerance: acid to alkaline
Soil moisture: tolerates moderate drought
Salt tolerance: low
Notes: variegated foliage often reverts to green
as plant grows older; has escaped cultivation,
especially in the panhandle of Florida and
southeastern U.S.

Botanical name: *Magnolia kobus* var. *stellata*
Common name: Star Magnolia
Hardiness zones: 5A-8B
Uses: accent
Florida native: no
Plant type: deciduous small tree or shrub
Mature size: 10-15 feet tall and wide
Flower: white or pink; showy in late winter or spring
Light requirement: full sun to part shade
Soil pH tolerance: acid to slightly alkaline
Soil moisture: tolerates moderate drought
Salt tolerance: none
Notes: many cultivars available with white or pink flowers

Botanical name: *Mahonia fortunei*
Common name: Fortune's Mahonia
Hardiness zones: 7B-9B
Uses: foundation; border; mass planting; accent
Florida native: no
Plant type: evergreen shrub
Mature size: 3-4 feet tall and wide
Flower: yellow; somewhat showy in spring, fall, winter
Light requirement: part shade to full shade
Soil pH tolerance: acid to slightly alkaline
Soil moisture: tolerates moderate drought
Salt tolerance: none
Notes: requires no maintenance to keep in bounds; powdery mildew occasionally coats foliage with white

Botanical name: *Mallotonia gnaphalodes*
Common name: Sea-Lavender
Hardiness zones: 10B-11
Uses: dune stabilization; border; mass planting
Florida native: yes
Plant type: evergreen shrub
Mature size: 2-5 feet tall by 6-20 feet wide
Flower: creamy white; somewhat showy in fall, winter
Light requirement: full sun
Soil pH tolerance: acid to alkaline
Soil moisture: tolerates drought
Salt tolerance: exceptionally high
Notes: bluish foliage makes this a winner, especially along beaches

Botanical name: *Malpighia glabra*
Common name: Barbados Cherry
Hardiness zones: 9B-11
Uses: bonsai; accent; container or planter; hedge; small tree; fruit
Florida native: no
Plant type: evergreen shrub or tree
Mature size: 10-12 feet tall and wide
Flower: pink; showy in summer
Light requirement: full sun to part shade
Soil pH tolerance: acid to slightly alkaline
Soil moisture: tolerates drought
Salt tolerance: moderate
Notes: wonderful fruit tree for small yard

Botanical name: *Malvaviscus arboreus*
Common name: Turk's Cap, Wax Mallow
Hardiness zones: 9A-11
Uses: border; attracts hummingbirds; accent
Florida native: no
Plant type: evergreen shrub
Mature size: 8-12 feet tall by 10-15 feet wide
Flower: red or pink; flowers year-round, especially in fall
Light requirement: full sun to part shade
Soil pH tolerance: acid to slightly alkaline
Soil moisture: tolerates moderate drought and poor drainage
Salt tolerance: moderate
Notes: striking red flowers cover plant for six months

Botanical name: *Michelia doltsopa* x *figo* 'Allspice'
Common name: 'Allspice' Banana Shrub
Hardiness zones: 8B-10B
Uses: accent; espalier; screen
Florida native: no
Plant type: evergreen shrub
Mature size: 15-20 feet tall by 6-15 feet wide
Flower: white; fragrant and showy in spring
Light requirement: full sun to part shade
Soil pH tolerance: acid
Soil moisture: tolerates moderate drought
Salt tolerance: low
Notes: requires regular attention because scales infest the brown-backed foliage; open canopy provides a light, airy effect; flower buds often killed by cold weather as they open

Botanical name: *Michelia figo*
Common name: Banana Shrub
Hardiness zones: 7B-10B
Uses: container or planter; accent; espalier; screen; border
Florida native: no
Plant type: evergreen shrub
Mature size: 10-20 feet tall by 6-15 feet wide
Flower: yellowish white; fragrant and showy in spring
Light requirement: full sun to part shade
Soil pH tolerance: acid
Soil moisture: tolerates moderate drought
Salt tolerance: low
Notes: scales regularly infest foliage

Botanical name: *Miscanthus sinensis* cultivars
Common name: Japanese Silver Grass
Hardiness zones: 4A-9B
Uses: mass planting; perennial border; screen; accent
Florida native: no
Plant type: ornamental grass
Mature size: 5-6 feet tall and wide
Flower: silvery white; showy in summer, fall
Light requirement: full sun
Soil pH tolerance: acid to slightly alkaline
Soil moisture: tolerates moderate drought and poor drainage
Salt tolerance: none
Notes: substitute for Pampas Grass on residential landscapes because Silver Grass is smaller and more delicate; plants may invade nearby landscapes

Botanical name: *Muhlenbergia capillaris*
Common name: Hair Awn Muhly Grass
Hardiness zones: 7A-11
Uses: dune stabilization; perennial border; accent; mass planting
Florida native: yes
Plant type: ornamental grass
Mature size: 3-5 feet tall by 3 feet wide
Flower: creamy white; showy red seeds in fall
Light requirement: full sun
Soil pH tolerance: acid to alkaline
Soil moisture: tolerates drought and poor drainage
Salt tolerance: high
Notes: versatile grass for many different soil types

Botanical name: *Murraya paniculata*
Common name: Orange-Jasmine, Chalcas
Hardiness zones: 9B-11
Uses: screen; container or planter; hedge; small tree
Florida native: no
Plant type: evergreen shrub; small tree
Mature size: 8-12 feet tall and wide
Flower: white; fragrant and periodically showy throughout the year
Light requirement: full sun to part shade
Soil pH tolerance: acid to alkaline
Soil moisture: tolerates drought
Salt tolerance: none
Notes: commonly used hedge with showy, red fruit

Botanical name: *Myrcianthes fragrans*
Common name: Simpson's Stopper, Twinberry
Hardiness zones: 9B-11
Uses: hedge; screen; attracts butterflies; small tree
Florida native: yes
Plant type: evergreen shrub or tree
Mature size: 20-30 feet tall by 15-20 feet wide
Flower: white; showy periodically throughout the year
Light requirement: full sun to full shade
Soil pH tolerance: acid to alkaline
Soil moisture: tolerates drought and poor drainage
Salt tolerance: high
Notes: bark shows off nicely when trained into small tree

Botanical name: *Myrica cerifera*
Common name: Southern Wax-myrtle, Southern Bayberry
Hardiness zones: 7B-11
Uses: screen; hedge; accent; small tree
Florida native: yes
Plant type: evergreen shrub or tree
Mature size: 15-20 feet tall and wide
Flower: inconspicuous
Light requirement: full sun to full shade
Soil pH tolerance: acid to alkaline
Soil moisture: tolerates moderate drought and poor drainage
Salt tolerance: high
Notes: short-lived; fruits appear on female plants only and attract wildlife; susceptible to disease, especially when pruned

Botanical name: *Nandina domestica*
Common name: Nandina, Heavenly Bamboo
Hardiness zones: 6B-10B
Uses: screen; container or planter; mass plant-
    ing; accent (can invade nearby landscapes)
Florida native: no   **INVASIVE**
Plant type: evergreen shrub
Mature size: 6-8 feet tall by 2-3 feet wide
Flower: white; showy in spring
Light requirement: full sun to part shade
Soil pH tolerance: acid to slightly alkaline
Soil moisture: tolerates moderate drought
Salt tolerance: low
Notes: red fruits attract birds and squirrels;
dwarf selections make good ground covers;
spreads by seeds and rhizomes; naturalized in
some wooded areas in north Florida

Botanical name: *Nerium oleander*
Common name: Oleander
Hardiness zones: 9A-11
Uses: screen; accent; container or planter;
    hedge; small tree
Florida native: no
Plant type: evergreen shrub or tree
Mature size: 3-15 feet tall and wide
Flower: red, pink, and orange; showy
    year-round
Light requirement: full sun to part shade
Soil pH tolerance: acid to alkaline
Soil moisture: tolerates drought
Salt tolerance: moderate
Notes: dwarf selections are best as shrubs; all
parts of plant are poisonous

Botanical name: *Nerium oleander* 'Petite Pink'
Common name: Dwarf Oleander, Petite
    Pink Oleander
Hardiness zones: 9A-11
Uses: container or planter; hedge; foundation;
    border; mass planting
Florida native: no
Plant type: evergreen shrub
Mature size: 4-6 feet tall by 5-8 feet wide
Flower: pink; showy year-round
Light requirement: full sun to part shade
Soil pH tolerance: acid to alkaline
Soil moisture: tolerates drought
Salt tolerance: high
Notes: space 4 feet apart in full sun to form
solid mass of color; plant is poisonous

Botanical name: *Opuntia* spp.
Common name: Prickly-Pear Cactus
Hardiness zones: 3B-11
Uses: accent; mass planting
Florida native: yes
Plant type: evergreen shrub
Mature size: 3-20 feet tall by 3-15 feet wide
Flower: yellow; showy in summer
Light requirement: full sun
Soil pH tolerance: acid to slightly alkaline
Soil moisture: tolerates drought
Salt tolerance: high
Notes: do not irrigate once established; spines are barbed and inflict pain as they meet flesh

Botanical name: *Osmanthus fragrans* *corner*
Common name: Sweet Osmanthus, Tea-Olive
Hardiness zones: 7B-9B
Uses: hedge; screen; accent
Florida native: no
Plant type: evergreen shrub
Mature size: 15-20 feet tall by 10-15 feet wide
Flower: creamy white; highly fragrant and
somewhat showy in fall and winter
Light requirement: full sun to part shade
Soil pH tolerance: acid
Soil moisture: tolerates moderate drought
Salt tolerance: low
Notes: perfumes garden during winter months; highly recommended

Botanical name: *Osmunda regalis*
Common name: Royal Fern
Hardiness zones: 3A-10B
Uses: mass planting; ground cover; accent
Florida native: yes
Plant type: fern
Mature size: 2-3 feet tall by 1-2 feet wide
Flower: spores are borne on a central stalk
Light requirement: part shade to full shade
Soil pH tolerance: acid to slightly alkaline
Soil moisture: drought sensitive; tolerates poor
drainage
Salt tolerance: none
Notes: delicate fern for wet, partly shaded
location

Botanical name: *Pachystachys lutea*
Common name: Golden Shrimp Plant
Hardiness zones: 9B-11
Uses: container or planter; hedge; foundation; perennial border; mass planting; accent
Florida native: no
Plant type: evergreen shrub
Mature size: 2-3 feet tall and wide
Flower: yellow; showy except in winter
Light requirement: full sun to part shade
Soil pH tolerance: acid to slightly alkaline
Soil moisture: drought sensitive
Salt tolerance: low
Notes: showy accent for prominent location; useful perennial in north Florida

Botanical name: *Pennisetum alopecuroides*
Common name: Chinese Fountain Grass
Hardiness zones: 5A-9B
Uses: mass planting; container or planter; accent; perennial border; cut flowers
Florida native: no
Plant type: ornamental grass
Mature size: 3-4 feet tall and wide
Flower: creamy white and pink; showy in summer and fall
Light requirement: full sun
Soil pH tolerance: acid to slightly alkaline
Soil moisture: tolerates drought
Salt tolerance: none
Notes: refined, fine-textured grass for sunny location; seedlings can be found germinating in nearby landscapes

Botanical name: *Pennisetum setaceum*
Common name: Tender Fountain Grass, Fountain Grass
Hardiness zones: 8B-10B
Uses: mass planting; container or planter; accent; border; cut flowers
Florida native: no
Plant type: ornamental grass
Mature size: 3-4 feet tall and wide
Flower: creamy white to red; showy in summer, fall
Light requirement: full sun
Soil pH tolerance: acid to slightly alkaline
Soil moisture: tolerates some drought
Salt tolerance: none
Notes: red-leaved selection most popular in certain regions; may escape cultivation; often lacks vigor unless irrigated

Botanical name: *Pentas lanceolata*
Common name: Pentas
Hardiness zones: 8B-11
Uses: accent; perennial border; container or planter; cut flowers; attracts hummingbirds and butterflies
Florida native: no
Plant type: annual or perennial
Mature size: 3 feet tall and wide
Flower: red or pink; showy except in winter
Light requirement: full sun to part shade
Soil pH tolerance: acid
Soil moisture: drought sensitive
Salt tolerance: low
Notes: easy to grow; dependable flowering plant for any garden

Botanical name: *Philodendron selloum*
Common name: Selloum
Hardiness zones: 8B-11
Uses: container or planter; accent; indoors
Florida native: no
Plant type: evergreen shrub
Mature size: 6-8 feet tall by 8-12 feet wide
Flower: inconspicuous
Light requirement: full sun to full shade
Soil pH tolerance: acid to slightly alkaline
Soil moisture: tolerates moderate drought and poor drainage
Salt tolerance: low
Notes: not suited to many residential landscapes because of large size

Botanical name: *Photinia x fraseri*
Common name: Fraser Photinia
Hardiness zones: 7B-9B
Uses: overused; hedge; screen; container or planter; small tree
Florida native: no
Plant type: evergreen shrub; small tree
Mature size: 12-18 feet tall by 8-12 feet wide
Flower: white; showy in summer
Light requirement: full sun
Soil pH tolerance: acid to slightly alkaline
Soil moisture: tolerates drought
Salt tolerance: high
Notes: provides nice flower display when unclipped; this is a high-maintenance plant because foliage usually is infected with fungus, especially in a shaded location

Botanical name: *Pittosporum tobira*
Common name: Japanese Pittosporum
Hardiness zones: 8A-11
Uses: dune stabilization; screen; hedge; container or planter
Florida native: no
Plant type: evergreen shrub
Mature size: 8-12 feet tall by 12-18 feet wide
Flower: white; fragrant and somewhat showy in late spring or summer
Light requirement: full sun
Soil pH tolerance: acid to alkaline
Soil moisture: tolerates drought; requires well-drained soil
Salt tolerance: high
Notes: versatile plant for all but wet locations; best suited for along the coast

Botanical name: *Pittosporum tobira* 'Variegata'
Common name: Variegated Pittosporum
Hardiness zones: 8A-11
Uses: dune stabilization; screen; hedge; mass planting; container or planter
Florida native: no **Plant type:** evergreen shrub
Mature size: 8-10 feet tall and wide
Flower: white; fragrant and showy in spring
Light requirement: full sun to part shade
Soil pH tolerance: acid to alkaline
Soil moisture: tolerates drought; requires well-drained soil
Salt tolerance: high
Notes: roots rot in wet soil; variegated foliage makes this a popular plant; best suited for along the coast

Botanical name: *Platycladus orientalis*
Common name: Arborvitae
Hardiness zones: 6A-10A
Uses: accent; screen
Florida native: no
Plant type: evergreen shrub
Mature size: 12-15 feet tall and wide
Flower: inconspicuous
Light requirement: full sun to part shade
Soil pH tolerance: acid
Soil moisture: tolerates drought
Salt tolerance: low
Notes: set back away from walks and drives to allow for spreading habit

Botanical name: *Plumbago auriculata*
Common name: Plumbago, Cape Plumbago
Hardiness zones: 9A-11
Uses: foundation; perennial border; mass
    planting; container or planter; hedge;
    attracts butterflies
Florida native: no
Plant type: viny, evergreen shrub
Mature size: 6-8 feet tall and wide
Flower: blue or white; showy except in winter
Light requirement: full sun to part shade
Soil pH tolerance: acid to slightly alkaline
Soil moisture: tolerates moderate drought
Salt tolerance: moderate
Notes: viny habit can be controlled with
regular clipping

Botanical name: *Podocarpus macrophyllus*
Common name: Yew Podocarpus, Japanese
    Yew
Hardiness zones: 8B-11
Uses: screen; hedge; espalier; indoors; tree
Florida native: no
Plant type: medium-sized, evergreen tree
Mature size: 30-40 feet tall by 20-25 feet wide
Flower: inconspicuous
Light requirement: full sun to mostly shaded
Soil pH tolerance: acid to alkaline
Soil moisture: tolerates drought
Salt tolerance: high
Notes: good hedge for mostly shaded location;
fruit is edible and juicy

Botanical name: *Polyscias pinnata*
Common name: Balfour Aralia
Hardiness zones: 10B-11
Uses: container or planter; hedge; perennial
    border; accent; cut foliage/twigs; indoors
Florida native: no
Plant type: evergreen shrub
Mature size: 6-10 feet tall by 2-4 feet wide
Flower: inconspicuous
Light requirement: full sun to full shade
Soil pH tolerance: acid to slightly alkaline
Soil moisture: tolerates drought and poor
    drainage
Salt tolerance: moderate
Notes: an erect plant for a tight space

Botanical name: *Psychotria nervosa*
Common name: Wild-Coffee
Hardiness zones: 10B-11
Uses: container or planter; accent; hedge;
    espalier; foundation; border; mass planting
Florida native: yes
Plant type: evergreen shrub
Mature size: 4-10 feet tall and wide
Flower: white; nearly inconspicuous
Light requirement: full sun to full shade
Soil pH tolerance: acid to alkaline
Soil moisture: tolerates moderate drought
Salt tolerance: moderate
Notes: shiny, dark green foliage and bright red
fruit make this a wonderful addition to any
landscape

Botanical name: *Pyracantha coccinea*
Common name: Firethorn
Hardiness zones: 6A-10B
Uses: screen; hedge; espalier
Florida native: no
Plant type: evergreen shrub
Mature size: 8-18 feet tall and wide
Flower: white; showy in spring
Light requirement: full sun to part shade
Soil pH tolerance: acid to alkaline
Soil moisture: tolerates drought and poor
    drainage
Salt tolerance: high
Notes: bright orange fruit attracts attention in
the fall; lanky habit requires regular pruning to
maintain neat appearance; cultivars available
with red or yellow fruit

Botanical name: *Raphiolepis indica*
Common name: Indian Hawthorn
Hardiness zones: 8A-11
Uses: foundation; border; mass planting;
    container or planter; ground cover
Florida native: no
Plant type: evergreen shrub
Mature size: 3-6 feet tall and wide
Flower: pink or white; showy in spring
Light requirement: full sun for best growth
Soil pH tolerance: acid to alkaline
Soil moisture: tolerates moderate drought
Salt tolerance: high
Notes: select from disease-resistant cultivars
and plant in full sun to avoid serious foliage
disease; great shrub for the coast

Botanical name: *Raphiolepis umbellata*
Common name: Round-Leaf Hawthorn,
   Yedda Hawthorn
Hardiness zones: 8A-10B
Uses: screen; border; hedge; accent; container
   or planter
Florida native: no
Plant type: evergreen shrub
Mature size: 10-15 feet tall by 8-10 feet wide
Flower: pink; showy in early spring
Light requirement: full sun to part shade
Soil pH tolerance: acid to alkaline
Soil moisture: tolerates drought
Salt tolerance: high
Notes: allow plenty of room for this large shrub

Botanical name: *Rhapidophyllum hystrix*
Common name: Needle Palm
Hardiness zones: 8A-10B
Uses: accent; mass planting; border
Florida native: yes
Plant type: palm
Mature size: 6-8 feet tall by 6-10 feet wide
Flower: inconspicuous
Light requirement: full sun to full shade
Soil pH tolerance: acid to slightly alkaline
Soil moisture: tolerates drought
Salt tolerance: moderate
Notes: best in moist sites, but adapts to
drought; long needles arm the trunk

Botanical name: *Rhapis excelsa*
Common name: Lady Palm
Hardiness zones: 8B-11
Uses: foundation; screen; border; container or
   planter; accent; indoors
Florida native: no
Plant type: palm
Mature size: 6-12 feet tall by 3-12 feet wide
Flower: inconspicuous
Light requirement: mostly sunny to full shade
Soil pH tolerance: acid to alkaline
Soil moisture: tolerates moderate drought
Salt tolerance: none
Notes: fabulous accent indoors or out

Botanical name: *Rhododendron canescens*
Common name: Pink Pinxter Azalea, Florida-Honeysuckle
Hardiness zones: 6B-10A
Uses: border; mass planting; accent; attracts hummingbirds and butterflies when in flower   **Florida native:** yes
Plant type: deciduous shrub
Mature size: 8-12 feet tall by 6-10 feet wide
Flower: pink; very showy in spring
Light requirement: part shade
Soil pH tolerance: acid
Soil moisture: tolerates some drought
Salt tolerance: none
Notes: one of the prettiest azaleas for Florida landscapes; pinch tips after flowering to increase flower display next year

Botanical name: *Rhododendron* 'Fashion'
Common name: 'Fashion' Azalea
Hardiness zones: 7A-10A
Uses: border; mass planting; attracts butterflies; cut flowers; accent; foundation
Florida native: no
Plant type: evergreen shrub
Mature size: 4-6 feet tall and wide
Flower: salmon; showy in fall and winter
Light requirement: part shade
Soil pH tolerance: acid
Soil moisture: tolerates some drought
Salt tolerance: none
Notes: flowers from November through March

Botanical name: *Rhododendron* 'George Taber'
Common name: 'George Taber' Azalea
Hardiness zones: 8A-10B
Uses: border; mass planting; accent; attracts butterflies; cut flowers; foundation
Florida native: no
Plant type: evergreen shrub
Mature size: 10-12 feet tall by 8-10 feet wide
Flower: pink; showy in late winter to early spring
Light requirement: part shade
Soil pH tolerance: acid
Soil moisture: tolerates moderate drought
Salt tolerance: none
Notes: commonly seen throughout Florida

Botanical name: *Russelia equisetiformis*
Common name: Firecracker Plant
Hardiness zones: 9B-11
Uses: container or planter; accent; mass
    planting; cascades down a wall
Florida native: no
Plant type: evergreen shrub
Mature size: 4-6 feet tall by 6-12 feet wide
Flower: red; showy year-round
Light requirement: full sun
Soil pH tolerance: acid to alkaline
Soil moisture: tolerates drought
Salt tolerance: moderate
Notes: good accent plant

Botanical name: *Sanchezia* spp.
Common name: Sanchezia
Hardiness zones: 10B-11
Uses: container or planter; accent
Florida native: no
Plant type: evergreen shrub
Mature size: 4-7 feet tall and wide
Flower: red; showy in summer and fall
Light requirement: full sun to part shade
Soil pH tolerance: acid to slightly alkaline
Soil moisture: drought sensitive
Salt tolerance: low
Notes: large foliage and bright red flowers lend
tropical effect to any landscape

Botanical name: *Sansevieria trifasciata*
Common name: Snake Plant, Mother-in-
    Law's Tongue
Hardiness zones: 9B-11
Uses: mass planting; accent; container or
    planter; indoors
Florida native: no
Plant type: perennial
Mature size: 3-5 feet tall by 2-3 feet wide
Flower: white; showy
Light requirement: full sun to full shade
Soil pH tolerance: acid to alkaline
Soil moisture: tolerates drought
Salt tolerance: high
Notes: adapts to any soil that drains well; best
as house plant or garden accent

Botanical name: *Scaevola frutescens* (= *S. sericea*)
Common name: Scaevola, Beach Naupaka
Hardiness zones: 10A-11
Uses: dune stabilization; border; mass planting; foundation; hedge
Florida native: no   **INVASIVE**
Plant type: evergreen shrub
Mature size: 5-10 feet tall and wide
Flower: inconspicuous
Light requirement: full sun to part shade
Soil pH tolerance: acid to alkaline
Soil moisture: tolerates drought
Salt tolerance: exceptionally high
Notes: soft, light green foliage makes this well suited for garden; plant invades coastal landscapes; escaped from cultivation on coasts in south Florida

Botanical name: *Scaevola plumieri*
Common name: Inkberry
Hardiness zones: 10A-11
Uses: dune stabilization; border; mass planting; foundation; reclamation; ground cover
Florida native: yes
Plant type: evergreen shrub
Mature size: 2-3 feet tall by 3-8 feet wide
Flower: inconspicuous
Light requirement: full sun to part shade
Soil pH tolerance: acid to alkaline
Soil moisture: tolerates drought
Salt tolerance: very high
Notes: small shrub adapted for beach

Botanical name: *Schaefferia frutescens*
Common name: Florida Boxwood
Hardiness zones: 10B-11
Uses: container or planter; hedge; espalier; screen; border
Florida native: yes
Plant type: evergreen shrub
Mature size: 15-25 feet tall by 10-15 feet wide
Flower: inconspicuous
Light requirement: full sun to part shade
Soil pH tolerance: acid to alkaline
Soil moisture: tolerates drought
Salt tolerance: moderate
Notes: small foliage makes this well suited for clipping into hedge

Botanical name: *Schefflera arboricola*
Common name: Dwarf Schefflera
Hardiness zones: 9B-11
Uses: screen; hedge; accent; container or
  planter; border; espalier; indoors
Florida native: no
Plant type: evergreen shrub
Mature size: 8-15 feet tall by 6-12 feet wide
Flower: white; showy in spring
Light requirement: full sun to full shade
Soil pH tolerance: acid to slightly alkaline
Soil moisture: tolerates moderate drought and
  poor drainage
Salt tolerance: low
Notes: bright orange fruit fills upper canopy;
makes good hedge

Botanical name: *Senna polyphylla*
Common name: Senna, Desert-Cassia
Hardiness zones: 10A-11
Uses: container or planter; accent; perennial
  border; attracts butterflies
Florida native: no
Plant type: semi-evergreen shrub
Mature size: 6-9 feet tall and wide
Flower: yellow; showy except in winter
Light requirement: full sun to part shade
Soil pH tolerance: acid to alkaline
Soil moisture: tolerates moderate drought
Salt tolerance: high
Notes: branches usually trained to emerge from
top of short trunk

Botanical name: *Serenoa repens*
Common name: Saw Palmetto
Hardiness zones: 8A-11
Uses: dune stabilization; mass planting; accent;
  ground cover; attracts butterflies
Florida native: yes
Plant type: palm
Mature size: 5-8 feet tall and wide
Flower: inconspicuous
Light requirement: full sun to full shade
Soil pH tolerance: acid to alkaline
Soil moisture: tolerates drought
Salt tolerance: high
Notes: spines along petiole make this a good
barrier planting; varieties with blue foliage are
very attractive

Botanical name: *Severinia buxifolia*
Common name: Boxthorn
Hardiness zones: 8B-10B
Uses: border; mass planting; foundation; hedge
Florida native: no
Plant type: evergreen shrub
Mature size: 5-12 feet tall by 4-6 feet wide
Flower: inconspicuous
Light requirement: full sun to part shade
Soil pH tolerance: acid to slightly alkaline
Soil moisture: tolerates drought
Salt tolerance: low
Notes: thorns on leaves make this a good hedge; black fruit prominent in winter

Botanical name: *Sophora tomentosa*
Common name: Necklace-Pod, Silver-Bush
Hardiness zones: 10A-11
Uses: mass planting; perennial border; accent; attracts butterflies
Florida native: yes
Plant type: evergreen shrub
Mature size: 6-10 feet tall by 8-12 feet wide
Flower: yellow; showy periodically throughout the year
Light requirement: full sun
Soil pH tolerance: acid to alkaline
Soil moisture: drought tolerant
Salt tolerance: high
Notes: can be trained into a small tree

Botanical name: *Spartina bakeri*
Common name: Marsh Grass
Hardiness zones: 8B-11
Uses: dune stabilization; reclamation; accent; border; edging; mass planting
Florida native: yes
Plant type: grass
Mature size: 3-4 feet tall and wide
Flower: creamy white; showy in fall
Light requirement: full sun
Soil pH tolerance: acid to slightly alkaline
Soil moisture: tolerates drought and poor drainage
Salt tolerance: high
Notes: adapts to many different soils; makes a soft, fine-textured accent

Botanical name: *Spiraea cantoniensis*
Common name: Reeve's Spiraea
Hardiness zones: 7A-9B
Uses: perennial border; mass planting; accent; container or planter
Florida native: no
Plant type: deciduous shrub
Mature size: 5-8 feet tall and wide
Flower: white; showy in spring
Light requirement: full sun
Soil pH tolerance: acid to slightly alkaline
Soil moisture: moderate drought
Salt tolerance: none
Notes: vase shape makes this an outstanding plant for an open landscape

Botanical name: *Strelitzia reginae*
Common name: Bird-of-Paradise
Hardiness zones: 10A-11
Uses: border; mass planting; container or planter; accent
Florida native: no
Plant type: herbaceous perennial
Mature size: 3-5 feet tall by 2-4 feet wide
Flower: orange and blue; showy in spring, summer
Light requirement: full sun to part shade
Soil pH tolerance: acid to slightly alkaline
Soil moisture: tolerates drought and poor drainage
Salt tolerance: none
Notes: upright habit and outstanding flower makes a great accent

Botanical name: *Strobilanthes dyeranus*
Common name: Persian Shield
Hardiness zones: 9A-11
Uses: container or planter; perennial border; accent; cut foliage/twigs
Florida native: no
Plant type: herbaceous perennial
Mature size: 4-5 feet tall and wide
Flower: inconspicuous
Light requirement: part shade to full shade
Soil pH tolerance: acid to slightly alkaline
Soil moisture: drought sensitive
Salt tolerance: none
Notes: grown as a perennial in northern Florida; purple foliage makes this a winner in any shady landscape

Botanical name: *Suriana maritima*
Common name: Bay-Cedar
Hardiness zones: 10B-11
Uses: dune stabilization; container or planter; hedge; mass planting; perennial border; attracts butterflies
Florida native: yes
Plant type: evergreen shrub
Mature size: 5-20 feet tall by 5-10 feet wide
Flower: yellow; inconspicuous
Light requirement: full sun
Soil pH tolerance: acid to alkaline
Soil moisture: drought tolerant
Salt tolerance: exceptionally high
Notes: beach plant adapted to nonirrigated landscapes inland

Botanical name: *Syzygium paniculatum*
Common name: Brush Cherry
Hardiness zones: 10A-11
Uses: bonsai; container or planter; hedge; screen
Florida native: no
Plant type: evergreen shrub
Mature size: 12-20 feet tall by 8-15 feet wide
Flower: inconspicuous
Light requirement: full sun to part shade
Soil pH tolerance: acid to alkaline
Soil moisture: drought tolerant
Salt tolerance: high
Notes: small leaves and tight growing habit make this well suited for a hedge

Botanical name: *Tabernaemontana divaricata*
Common name: Crape-Jasmine, Pinwheel Flower
Hardiness zones: 10B-11
Uses: mass planting; specimen; container or planter; hedge; foundation
Florida native: no
Plant type: evergreen shrub
Mature size: 6-10 feet tall and wide
Flower: white; slightly fragrant and showy year-round
Light requirement: full sun to part shade
Soil pH tolerance: acid to alkaline
Soil moisture: drought sensitive
Salt tolerance: moderate
Notes: snow-white flowers contrast with shiny, dark green foliage

Your Florida Guide to Shrubs

Botanical name: *Tecoma stans*
Common name: Yellow-Elder, Yellow
    Trumpet-Flower
Hardiness zones: 10A-11
Uses: container or planter; specimen; espalier;
    small tree
Florida native: no
Plant type: large, evergreen shrub or tree
Mature size: 12-20 feet tall and wide
Flower: yellow; showy year-round
Light requirement: full sun
Soil pH tolerance: acid to alkaline
Soil moisture: drought tolerant
Salt tolerance: moderate
Notes: canary yellow flowers fill the canopy
except in winter

Botanical name: *Tecomaria capensis*
Common name: Cape Honeysuckle
Hardiness zones: 9B-11
Uses: mass planting; accent; hedge; perennial
    border; container or planter; espalier;
    attracts hummingbirds
Florida native: no
Plant type: viny, evergreen shrub
Mature size: variable height by 6-10 feet wide
Flower: orange; showy year-round
Light requirement: full sun
Soil pH tolerance: acid to alkaline
Soil moisture: moderate drought
Salt tolerance: high
Notes: spectacular flowers make this a wonder-
ful addition to the landscape; only regular
trimming keeps this viny shrub within bounds

Botanical name: *Ternstroemia gymnanthera*
Common name: Cleyera, Japanese
    Ternstroemia
Hardiness zones: 7A-10B
Uses: screen; border; hedge
Florida native: no
Plant type: evergreen shrub
Mature size: 12-20 feet tall by 5-10 feet wide
Flower: white; showy in spring
Light requirement: part shade to full shade
Soil pH tolerance: acid to slightly alkaline
Soil moisture: moderate drought
Salt tolerance: none
Notes: glossy, new foliage gives this shrub a
touch of elegance in the landscape

Botanical name: *Tetrazygia bicolor*
Common name: Florida Tetrazygia
Hardiness zones: 10B-11
Uses: hedge; screen; border
Florida native: yes
Plant type: evergreen shrub
Mature size: 10-30 feet tall by 10 feet wide
Flower: creamy white; showy in spring, summer
Light requirement: full sun to part shade
Soil pH tolerance: acid to alkaline
Soil moisture: drought tolerant
Salt tolerance: moderate
Notes: coarse foliage draws attention to this plant in the garden

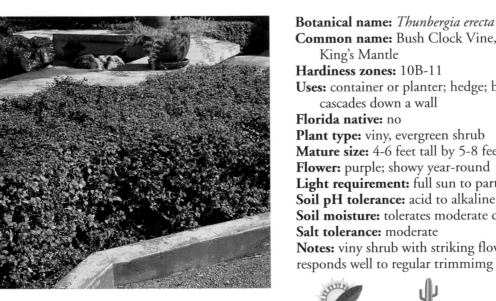

Botanical name: *Thunbergia erecta*
Common name: Bush Clock Vine, King's Mantle
Hardiness zones: 10B-11
Uses: container or planter; hedge; border; cascades down a wall
Florida native: no
Plant type: viny, evergreen shrub
Mature size: 4-6 feet tall by 5-8 feet wide
Flower: purple; showy year-round
Light requirement: full sun to part shade
Soil pH tolerance: acid to alkaline
Soil moisture: tolerates moderate drought
Salt tolerance: moderate
Notes: viny shrub with striking flowers that responds well to regular trimmimg

Botanical name: *Tibouchina* spp.
Common name: Princess-Flower
Hardiness zones: 10A-11
Uses: container or planter; accent; perennial border
Florida native: no
Plant type: evergreen shrub
Mature size: 8-15 feet tall and wide
Flower: purple; showy in summer, fall
Light requirement: full sun to part shade
Soil pH tolerance: acid to slightly alkaline
Soil moisture: drought sensitive
Salt tolerance: none
Notes: grown as a woody perennial in north Florida

Botanical name: *Tripsacum dactyloides*

Common name: Fakahatchee Grass, Eastern Gamma Grass, Gamma Grass

Hardiness zones: 5A-11

Uses: reclamation; accent; border; mass planting

Florida native: yes

Plant type: ornamental grass

Mature size: 5-7 feet tall and wide

Flower: inconspicuous

Light requirement: full sun to part shade

Soil pH tolerance: acid to slightly alkaline

Soil moisture: tolerates moderate drought and poor drainage

Salt tolerance: low

Notes: adapted to many soils; use instead of Pampas Grass because it's smaller, prettier and native to Florida

Botanical name: *Tripsacum floridana*

Common name: Florida Gamma Grass, Dwarf Fakahatchee Grass

Hardiness zones: 8A-11

Uses: accent; border; mass planting; container or planter

Florida native: yes

Plant type: ornamental grass

Mature size: 3-4 feet tall by 4-6 feet wide

Flower: inconspicuous

Light requirement: full sun to part shade

Soil pH tolerance: acid to slightly alkaline

Soil moisture: tolerates moderate drought and poor drainage

Salt tolerance: low

Notes: foliage blows easily in light breezes providing a softening effect in the landscape

Botanical name: *Turnera ulmifolia*

Common name: Yellow-Alder

Hardiness zones: 9A-11

Uses: container or planter; foundation; border; mass planting; ground cover; attracts butterflies

Florida native: no

Plant type: evergreen shrub

Mature size: 2-3 feet tall and wide

Flower: yellow; showy year-round

Light requirement: full sun to part shade

Soil pH tolerance: acid to alkaline

Soil moisture: tolerates moderate drought

Salt tolerance: high

Notes: can escape cultivation and become weedy

Botanical name: *Viburnum obovatum*
Common name: Blackhaw, Walter Viburnum
Hardiness zones: 7A-10B
Uses: container or planter; espalier; hedge; screen; border; attracts butterflies; small tree
Florida native: yes
Plant type: evergreen shrub or tree
Mature size: 8-25 feet tall by 6-10 feet wide
Flower: white; showy in spring
Light requirement: full sun to part shade
Soil pH tolerance: acid to alkaline
Soil moisture: tolerates drought and poor drainage
Salt tolerance: moderate
Notes: makes a great hedge because of its small leaves

Botanical name: *Viburnum odoratissimum*
Common name: Sweet Viburnum
Hardiness zones: 8B-10A
Uses: screen; hedge; container or planter; accent; street tree
Florida native: no
Plant type: large shrub or tree
Mature size: 20-30 feet tall by 15-25 feet wide
Flower: white; showy in spring
Light requirement: full sun to partial shade
Soil pH tolerance: acid to alkaline
Soil moisture: tolerates drought
Salt tolerance: low
Notes: although commonly planted as a hedge, it is too big for this purpose

Botanical name: *Viburnum suspensum*
Common name: Sandankwa Viburnum
Hardiness zones: 8B-10B
Uses: foundation; screen; border; container or planter; hedge
Florida native: no
Plant type: evergreen shrub
Mature size: 6-10 feet tall by 4-7 feet wide
Flower: inconspicuous
Light requirement: full sun to part shade
Soil pH tolerance: acid to alkaline
Soil moisture: tolerates moderate drought and poor drainage
Salt tolerance: low
Notes: dense growth habit and dark green foliage make this a popular hedge

Botanical name: *Viburnum tinus*
Common name: Laurestinus Viburnum
Hardiness zones: 7A-9B
Uses: screen; hedge; border; accent
Florida native: no
Plant type: evergreen shrub
Mature size: 8-12 feet tall by 4-6 feet wide
Flower: white; showy in spring
Light requirement: full sun to part shade
Soil pH tolerance: acid to slightly alkaline
Soil moisture: tolerates moderate drought
Salt tolerance: none
Notes: provides vertical accent in landscape

Botanical name: *Vitex agnus-castus*
Common name: Chaste Tree
Hardiness zones: 7B-11
Uses: accent; container or planter; small tree
Florida native: no
Plant type: deciduous shrub or tree
Mature size: 10-15 feet tall and wide
Flower: purple and lavender; showy in spring, summer
Light requirement: full sun to part shade
Soil pH tolerance: acid to alkaline
Soil moisture: tolerates drought
Salt tolerance: moderate
Notes: nice accent while in flower; white cultivar available

Botanical name: *Yucca aloifolia*
Common name: Spanish Bayonet, Aloe Yucca
Hardiness zones: 6A-11
Uses: mass planting; barrier; perennial border; accent; attracts butterflies
Florida native: yes
Plant type: evergreen shrub
Mature size: 10-15 feet tall by 3-5 feet wide
Flower: white; showy in spring, summer
Light requirement: full sun to part shade
Soil pH tolerance: acid to alkaline
Soil moisture: tolerates drought
Salt tolerance: high
Notes: fabulous accent; locate away from children because of sharp terminal spine on each leaf

Botanical name: *Yucca filamentosa*
Common name: Adam's Needle, Filamentose Yucca
Hardiness zones: 7B-10B
Uses: mass planting; perennial border; accent; attracts butterflies
Florida native: yes
Plant type: evergreen shrub
Mature size: 3 feet tall and wide
Flower: white; showy in spring
Light requirement: full sun to full shade
Soil pH tolerance: acid to alkaline
Soil moisture: tolerates drought
Salt tolerance: high
Notes: fabulous accent for any landscape, with or without irrigation

Botanical name: *Yucca gloriosa*
Common name: Spanish Dagger, Mound-Lily Yucca
Hardiness zones: 6A-11
Uses: mass planting; accent; attracts butterflies
Florida native: yes
Plant type: evergreen shrub
Mature size: 6-8 feet tall by 4-8 feet wide
Flower: showy in spring, summer
Light requirement: full sun to part shade
Soil pH tolerance: acid to alkaline
Soil moisture: tolerates drought
Salt tolerance: high
Notes: large yucca best saved for large landscape site

Botanical name: *Zamia floridana*
Common name: Coontie
Hardiness zones: 8B-11
Uses: foundation; border; mass planting; accent; attracts butterflies
Florida native: yes
Plant type: evergreen shrub
Mature size: 2-4 feet tall by 3-5 feet wide
Flower: male cone 6 inches long by 1-2 inches wide; female cone to 8 inches tall by 4 inches wide
Light requirement: full sun to part shade
Soil pH tolerance: acid to alkaline
Soil moisture: tolerates drought
Salt tolerance: high
Notes: plant in mass for soft textured effect

Botanical name: *Zamia furfuracea*

Common name: Cardboard Plant, Cardboard Cycad

Hardiness zones: 9B-11

Uses: foundation; border; mass planting; container or planter; indoors; accent

Florida native: no

Plant type: evergreen shrub

Mature size: 3-5 feet tall by 5-8 feet wide

Flower: 4-inch-long, cylindrical male cone; 5-inch-long, ovoid female cone

Light requirement: full sun to part shade

Soil pH tolerance: acid to alkaline

Soil moisture: tolerates drought

Salt tolerance: high

Notes: fabulous accent when surrounded by low ground cover

Notes

. . . .

_____

_____

_____

_____

_____

_____

_____

_____

_____

_____

_____

_____

_____

Establishing plants

Strive to maintain constant moisture in the root ball, but avoid keeping it saturated. If planting during the warm part of the year, water the root ball every day for the first few weeks after planting. Gradually decrease the frequency of irrigation to every other day and then to every third day until shrubs are established (Table 6). Shrubs planted in cooler seasons can be watered less often. There is usually no need to water the soil outside the root ball because this soil dries slowly until roots grow into it.

If provided with regular irrigation, 1-gallon shrubs become established about 3 to 6 months after planting, and 7-gallon plants take about a year or slightly longer in the northern half of the state. Water applied under the canopy weekly through the second year after planting can help maintain vigorous growth. To encourage fast growth, you might consider this irrigation strategy until the shrubs are close to the desired size, then eliminate irrigation to slow down growth. In most landscapes, once shrubs are well established, they do not need to be watered except during drought or perhaps in the dry season.

Shrubs can benefit from a small amount of slow-release fertilizer applied to the top of the root ball 4 to 6 weeks after planting, but it is not needed for survival.

Table 6. Establishment time for shrubs.		
Plant size (container size)	Time to establish	Amount of irrigation to apply
1 gallon	3 to 6 months	1 quart
3 gallon	6 to 12 months	2 quarts
7 gallon	1 to 2 years	1 gallon

Maintaining shrubs

How shrubs are cared for not only determines how well they grow but also has an impact on energy and water consumption, and thus the environment. Apply enough water and fertilizer to keep them growing and healthy, but not so much as to waste water, encourage excessive growth, or pollute our lakes and waterways with fertilizer-contaminated runoff.

Watering
When to Water

Once shrubs are established, variables such as plant species, soil type, time of year, sunlight exposure, and weather conditions determine when shrubs should be watered and with how much water. Consequently it is difficult to offer specific watering procedures. However, the following guidelines should provide some general information.

Once shrubs have adapted to the conditions of the site, irrigation is most often needed in spring (May) and fall (October) when temperatures are typically high and rainfall amounts low. In many years, little irrigation is needed during the summer rainy period. Irrigate only when shrubs need water, as indicated by wilting leaves (Figure 15). Follow local water regulations that dictate irrigation days and hours. During the summer, if properly selected, established plants located in full sun need no water for a couple of weeks after a water application (including rainfall) of at least 3/4 inch of water. They can go

longer without water if planted in the shade or in soils of fine texture, such as marl or clay, as well as during the winter.

Shrubs should be watered early in the morning when wind and temperature levels are low. Irrigating during the late morning, at midday, or during the afternoon usually results in more water lost to evaporation. With overhead irrigation systems, unequal water distribution is also more likely

Figure 15. Some shrubs will demonstrate their need for water by wilting.

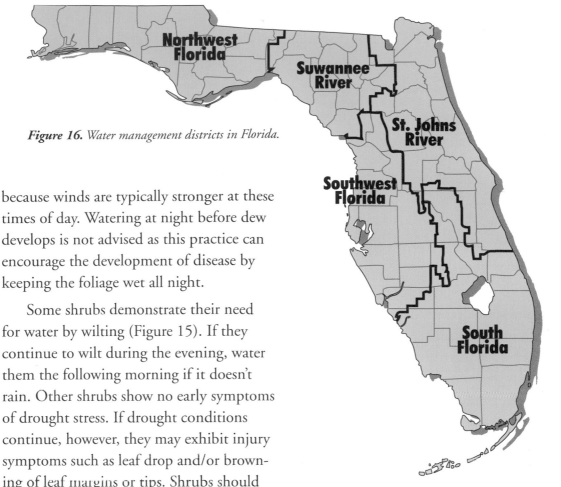

Figure 16. Water management districts in Florida.

because winds are typically stronger at these times of day. Watering at night before dew develops is not advised as this practice can encourage the development of disease by keeping the foliage wet all night.

Some shrubs demonstrate their need for water by wilting (Figure 15). If they continue to wilt during the evening, water them the following morning if it doesn't rain. Other shrubs show no early symptoms of drought stress. If drought conditions continue, however, they may exhibit injury symptoms such as leaf drop and/or browning of leaf margins or tips. Shrubs should be watered just before the appearance of injury symptoms. When you become familiar with your plants, you will be able to determine when they need water just by looking at them. Chances are, all shrubs in the landscape will not need to be watered on the same day. Only water those that appear to need it. Compared to using a time clock to schedule the irrigation, this is a much more efficient way to irrigate.

When you decide it is time to water, be sure to comply with local and regional water regulations set by your water management district (Figure 16). In many areas, irrigation is allowed only on certain days or during specified hours. Also check TV, radio, newspaper, or Internet services for local rain forecasts before irrigating. If a weather front is approaching with rain likely in the next day or two, don't turn on the irrigation. Established plants are unlikely to be damaged by another couple of days of drought. Monitor local rainfall with a simple rain gauge, and install and maintain an automatic rain switch on automatic irrigation systems. A rain switch prevents the irrigation system from operating when it's raining. You will save water by following these guidelines.

How Much Water to Apply

When watering established plants, soak the soil thoroughly. Frequent, light sprinklings waste water and do little to satisfy the water requirements of an established plant growing in hot, dry soil because water may not percolate through the mulch to the roots. Shrubs watered in this way could develop shallow root systems, increasing their susceptibility to damage if watering is interrupted for a few days.

For most of Florida's sandy soils, 1/2 to 3/4 inch of rainfall or irrigation is sufficient to wet the root zone. Because not all soils

Figure 17. *Measure water levels in containers placed in a sprinkler's spray pattern to determine amount of water being applied.*

and shrubs are alike, however, some adjustments in the amount of water applied may be necessary.

To determine when a hose-end or in-ground sprinkler system has delivered 3/4 inch of water, place cans or straight-sided cartons at intervals within the spray pattern (as shown in Figure 17) and continue watering until the average water level in the cans reaches 3/4 inch. Operate the irrigation system for this length of time each time you irrigate.

Watering Methods

Irrigation systems operate most efficiently if they don't wet the foliage of the plants. Water applied to the foliage is not used by the plant. Although not always practical, sprinkler heads and nozzles can sometimes be lowered to just above the ground surface so they throw water beneath the shrub canopy. This keeps most foliage dry and is usually appropriate for large shrubs because small ones often have foliage all the way to the ground. This lower foliage blocks the spray and in some instances could keep those plants farthest from the sprinkler too dry.

Although not commonly used, the most efficient and effective watering method currently in use is microirrigation, which is also known as drip or trickle irrigation (Figure 18). Microirrigation supplies small quantities of water directly to the mulch and soil through plastic

tubing located on or below the ground surface. Low-pressure emitters (i.e., nozzles that drip, spray or sprinkle) are attached to the plastic tubing and slowly release water into the soil around a plant. Wetting only the root zone results in dramatic water savings because less is evaporated. Microirrigation kits are available at many home and garden stores, and individual components of a system can be purchased at irrigation supply stores. More sophisticated systems can be designed and installed by a professional. Irrigation supply stores also carry what are known as retrofit kits for converting existing irrigation systems to microirrigation.

When microirrigating, you need to know which kind of emitter to install in a given location. With drip emitters, water will move laterally in sand only 10 to 12

Figure 18. *Microsprayers create a fan-shaped distribution of fine water droplets.*

Your Florida Guide to Shrubs

inches from the emitter. Drip emitters are ideal when such precision is desirable or for narrow strip plantings, such as along hedge rows (Figure 20). Because drip emitters are sometimes placed under mulch or buried in the soil, clogging may occur that is further magnified by the difficulty in detecting the problem. Because the action of drip emitters is not readily apparent, it is also difficult to know whether the system is irrigating excessively due to a hole in the tubing or oversight. Regular inspection is required to make sure that the drip emitters and the overall system are functioning as they should. In fact, all irrigation systems should be inspected for leaks and uniform coverage to ensure efficient operation.

On the whole, spray-jets (either microsprayers or microsprinklers) are more desirable than drip emitters for most Florida landscape applications. Because spray-jets can cover areas 3 to 20 feet in diameter, fewer emitters are needed. Not only is their action visible, but the greater flow rate of water through spray-jets (10 to 20 gallons per hour versus the drip emitter's .25 to 2 gallons per hour) makes them less susceptible to clogging. Microsprayers create a fan-shaped distribution of fine water droplets (Figure 18). These fan-jets perform well when used for directional spray and confined area applications. Shaping vanes, known as spokes, can be added to create streams of water called spoke-jets. A spoke-shaped application pattern works well for a single shrub. A deflection cap will confine the application to areas 2 to 5 feet in diameter. Some manufacturers have added spinner devices to create a sprinkler effect (Figure 19). These microsprinklers have more uniform water distribution than the fan-jets or spoke-jets and can provide excellent coverage.

Regardless of the emitter style, clogging can be a problem if the water supply is not filtered at the point it enters the irrigation system (Figure 21). Filters are easily in-

Figure 19. Microsprinklers have more uniform water distribution than microsprayers.

Figure 20. Drip emitters are well suited for narrow strip plantings and new plantings.

Figure 21. *Plants can die from drought stress if clogged emitters are not detected.*

Scheduling irrigation with a time clock is easy but wasteful. The time clock turns on the system in rain or sunshine, regardless of whether the plants need water. A sprinkler system with a time clock may be manually controlled by setting the time clock to the "off" position and switching the system on when the plants need water. The automatic position on the time clock is useful when you are away from home for more than a few days. By installing a shutoff device that overrides the system when rain falls, you can make the system operate even more efficiently. Soil-moisture sensors often require a lot of maintenance to remain accurate.

stalled in any irrigation system. It is especially recommended that water from wells be filtered. The safest and easiest way to maintain the emitters in a microirrigation system is to keep a small supply of clean backups on hand. Clogged devices can be easily replaced with clean units and then placed in a small container of cleaning fluid appropriate for the clogging material.

With systems other than microirrigation, water should be applied only as fast as the soil can absorb it. Using a hose with water pressure at full force can do more damage than good. Fast-flowing water carries away soil, exposing plant roots to direct sunlight. Watering with sprinklers is more efficient. Whether using a sprinkler attached to a hose or an automatic sprinkler system in the ground, the efficiency of the system depends on how well it is managed. A hose-end sprinkler may be placed anywhere in the landscape and allowed to run until it has delivered 3/4 inch of water. If the sprinkler is moved too soon, water may not wet the entire root zone. If the sprinkler runs too long, water will pass below the root zone and be wasted.

Irrigation systems may be operated automatically with a time clock or soil sensor, or they can be manually controlled.

Fertilization
Deciding if fertilization is needed

Fertilization of plants usually results in additional growth and production of leaves, stems, branches, and roots. Often this growth results in additional maintenance costs and more yard trimmings to be disposed of, so it is important to determine if growth is the result we want with our shrubs. Fertilizer is also useful for preventing nutrient deficiencies in acid-loving shrubs (Figure 22) improperly installed into soil with a high pH.

Figure 22. *Manganese deficiency in ixora.*

Fertilization is usually desirable when we are trying to establish newly planted shrubs. We normally want the new plants to get off to a quick start and grow rapidly so they fill the planted area. When this is the case, fertilize about 4 to 6 weeks after planting and then two to three times per year for the following 3 years or so. Two of the annual applications are normally scheduled around February and October for south Florida, March and September for north Florida. A third application can be made during the summer.

Soil Testing

Soil testing provides some information about the pH and nutritional status of soil and may aid in the detection of potential nutritional problems. Soil tests routinely measure soil pH and give an index of the available phosphorus and potassium. If you are prepared to modify your fertilization practices to fit specific fertilization recommendations based on a soil test, the following instructions on conducting soil sampling will be useful. However, if you plan on simply using one of the commonly recommended fertilizers, such as 12-4-8 or 16-4-8, there is no logical reason to go to the trouble of testing. Skip to the section on how much fertilizer to use (p. 92). However, using these commonly available fertilizers is often wasteful because few soils

in Florida require phosphorus applications to support healthy plants.

Test the soil area to be fertilized prior to purchasing fertilizer. Collect the sample(s) and send them to the lab a couple of months before you anticipate needing to fertilize. This allows ample time for the lab to get results back to you.

Obtain a composite soil sample by removing subsamples from 10 to 12 small holes dug throughout the sample area (e.g., the front yard of your home). To obtain the subsamples, carefully pull back mulch, grass, or ground covers to expose bare soil. With a hand trowel or shovel, dig small holes 6 inches deep, then remove a 1-inch-wide by 6-inch-deep slice of soil from the

Figure 23. *Soil testing can determine the pH and nutritional status of soil.*

side of each hole (Figure 23). Combine and mix the subsamples in a clean plastic bucket. You will use about a pint of this mixture as your sample. When various areas in the landscape have different soil types, receive different cultural practices, or contain plants that have distinctly different fertilization requirements, obtain separate

Table 7. Amounts of various commonly available fertilizers needed to fertilize shrubs and young trees.[1,2]

	Diameter of plant canopy in feet										
	2		4		6		8		10		12
	Diameter of area to be fertilized in feet[3]										
	3		6		9		12		15		18
Fertilizer	lbs	tbs[4]	lbs	tbs	lbs	tbs	lbs	cups[5]	lbs	cups	lbs
12-4-8	0.059	1.9	0.24	7.5	0.53	17.0	0.94	1.9	1.5	3.0	2.1	4.2
15-5-15	0.047	1.5	0.19	6.0	0.42	13.6	0.75	1.5	1.2	2.4	1.7	3.4
16-4-8	0.044	1.4	0.18	5.6	0.40	12.7	0.71	1.4	1.1	2.2	1.6	3.2
23-6-12	0.031	1.0	0.12	3.9	0.28	8.8	0.49	1.0	0.77	1.5	1.11	2.2
34-0-0	0.020	0.7	0.08	2.6	0.19	6.0	0.33	0.7	0.52	1.0	0.75	1.5

[1] The amounts of fertilizer indicated in this table were calculated on the rate of applying 1 pound of nitrogen per 1000 square feet.
[2] Spread this amount of fertilizer in a circle that is 1.5 times the diameter of the plant canopy.
[3] Diameter of plant canopy multiplied by 1.5.
[4] Approximate number of tablespoons of fertilizer for a given weight (lbs) of fertilizer.
[5] Approximate number of cups of fertilizer for a given weight (lbs) of fertilizer.

composite samples from each area. Often a 1/4- to 1-acre lot will have two or three areas that require separate sampling. Soil samples need to be sent immediately to a commercial laboratory, or check with your local county Cooperative Extension office.

How Much Fertilizer to Use

Once you have decided to fertilize, use Table 7 to determine the amount of fertilizer to apply to individual shrubs. In most instances, roots will ultimately extend quite a bit beyond the drip line, so the fertilized zone should be one and a half times the distance from the base of the plant to the outer edge of its branches.

The amount of fertilizer to apply to shrubs in a bed can be determined by calculating the area of the bed and then applying fertilizer at the rate of 1 pound of nitrogen per 1000 square feet of bed area. To calculate the area of a shrub bed (Figure 25), simply multiply the length of the bed by its width. It is easy to determine how much fertilizer to apply using information given on each bag of fertilizer (Figure 24). Dividing the nitrogen (N) content into 100 gives you the number of pounds of fertilizer to apply per 1000 square feet. You must then figure out how much

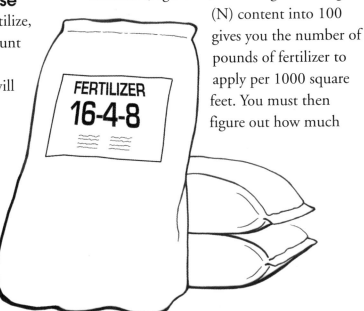

Figure 24. *Determine grade or analysis from the numbers. 16-4-8 means 16% nitrogen, 4% phosphate, and 8% potash.*

Figure 25.
Measure the length and width of a bed to calculate its area.

fertilizer to apply to the shrub bed. Because we give fertilizer recommendations on a 1000-square-feet basis, first divide the area of the bed by 1000. Multiply this result by the pounds of fertilizer needed per 1000 square feet. This gives you the total amount of fertilizer to apply to the bed (Figure 26).

What fertilizer to use

A complete fertilizer with a ratio of approximately 3:1:2 or 3:1:3 (e.g., 12-4-8 or 15-5-15) of nitrogen (N), phosphoric acid (P_2O_5) and potash (K_2O) is often recommended unless the soil test reveals that phosphorus and potassium are adequate. Similar analysis fertilizers such as 16-4-8 (4:1:2) also can be used. However, phosphorus is usually not needed in most of Florida's landscapes.

Many fertilizers are formulated for use on lawn grasses. Some of these, known as weed-and-feed fertilizers, may contain an herbicide that can damage shrubs. Read labels and carefully follow the directions.

Fertilizers that are "slow-release," "controlled-release," sulfur-coated, or that contain nitrogen as IBDU (isobutylidene diurea) or ureaformaldehyde have extended release periods compared to fertilizers that are readily water-soluble (Figure 27). Thirty to 50 percent of the nitrogen should be water-insoluble or slow-release so that plant roots can absorb the nitrogen over a long period of time.

A fertilizer containing 30 to 50 percent slow-release potassium is often recommended for south Florida or where soil

Figure 26. *Calculating amount of fertilizer needed.*

> ### As an example:
> - if your bed is 20'long x 10' wide,
> - the area of the bed is 20' x 10',
> - which equals 200 square feet.
>
> Let's say you purchased a 10-5-10 (N-P-K) fertilizer. The first of these three numbers is the percentage of nitrogen in the fertilizer. You would divide this number into 100, giving you 100 ÷ 10 = 10 pounds of 10-5-10 fertilizer per 1000 square feet of bed area. Divide the area of the bed, 200 square feet, by 1000, giving you a result of 0.2. Then multiply this number, 0.2, by the number of pounds of fertilizer per 1000 square feet that you previously calculated, which was 10 pounds. Because 0.2 x 10 = 2, you would spread 2 pounds of fertilizer over the entire bed area.

Figure 27. Controlled-release fertilizers have extended nutrient release periods compared to water-soluble fertilizers.

potassium is inadequate. A fertilizer containing magnesium may be needed if soils contain inadequate magnesium or if plants often exhibit magnesium deficiency symptoms.

Water-soluble fertilizers are less expensive than slow-release products. However, the components of a water-soluble fertilizer may leach quickly through the soil and past the roots, which is wasteful. In sandy, well-drained soils, the soluble fertilizer may move below the root system after only a few inches of rainfall or irrigation. In finer-textured marl, clay or muck soils, leaching will be slower, but runoff may be greater, which could contribute to pollution of the surface water.

Micronutrient deficiencies (Figures 28 and 29) can be corrected with foliar sprays if deficiencies are not severe; however, such correction is usually temporary and is not commonly used. Deficiencies may be prevented by applying a fertilizer with micronutrient supplements to the soil. This is particularly useful in landscapes in the southern part of the state but is also suited for azaleas and some other plants throughout the state.

Figure 28. Magnesium deficiancy in pittosporum.

Figure 29. Manganese deficiency in gardenia.

Where and how to apply fertilizer

Because of the naturally high oxygen concentrations near the soil surface, a plant's principal feeding roots are usually within the top 10 to 14 inches of soil. Many roots of mulched plants are located just beneath the mulch on the soil surface. Consequently, for maximum utilization, fertilizer should be applied to the surface of the soil or mulch. Since most small-diameter (feeder) roots are shallow, there is no need to inject or place fertilizer deep in the soil. However, shallow soil injections in compacted soil or on mounds, berms and slopes will reduce the amount of fertilizer runoff caused by irrigation or rain.

A large, aesthetically pleasing mulched area should be maintained around shrubs. This mulched area promotes faster shrub establishment by eliminating competition from grass roots for water and nutrients. Ground covers that are not as competitive as grass for water and nutrients can be planted near shrubs.

Pruning

Through selective removal of shoots and branches, pruning a shrub can maintain its health, reduce its size, and enhance fruiting, flowering or appearance. Pruning should be a part of your gardening routine and not delayed until the landscape is overgrown. An unpruned shrub can end up tall and leggy with little foliage close to the ground. In this condition it cannot be pruned to a desirable size or shape in a single pruning without causing severe damage to the plant. Instead, it must be pruned back gradually over a period of several years.

Proper shrub selection can eliminate many pruning requirements. Too often a shrub is selected for the landscape based on its current size and shape, rather than the size and shape it is likely to attain at maturity 5 or more years later. The homeowner or landscape manager may soon find it necessary to clip or prune shrubs frequently to keep them within bounds. It is less time-consuming and less costly to select and install the appropriate size shrub for the location to begin with. Consult the Shrub Selection Guide (p. 24) for the mature size of the shrub species you are considering for your landscape. If a shrub needs to be pruned several times each year to control size, it is quite likely the wrong species for its location.

Reasons for pruning

Although we tend to think of pruning as a measure for controlling the form of a shrub, shrubs may be pruned for a number of other reasons. Before pruning, determine which of the following benefits you hope to achieve through your efforts.

Health and Improved Vigor

Weekly inspection of your landscape is recommended to detect shrubs threatened

Figure 30a.
Properly pruned hedges create privacy but require regular clipping to keep them looking neat.

Figure 30b.
Shrubs pruned into geometric shapes are called topiaries.

by disease or infestation. Often insect, pest and disease problems can be "nipped in the bud" by the removal of dead, dying, damaged or infected plant parts. For example, if several branch tips are infested with aphids or scale, pruning and discarding the affected shoots can be an effective alternative to spraying with insecticides if the infestation is small and localized. Pruning to remove diseased or infested plant parts can also help stop a problem from spreading to neighboring shrubs.

Plant Size and Form

A common objective of pruning is to maintain or develop a desired size or form. As mentioned earlier, this reason for pruning can be largely eliminated by installing the proper species. Compact and dwarf shrubs are now widely available and are a good choice where small or low-growing plants are desired. Once plants grow to the size you want them to be, reduce the number of fertilizer applications and water infrequently to prevent shrubs from growing more rapidly than desired.

Always work with the natural form of a shrub. Frequent light prunings several times each year discourage undesirable

sprouting. Several light prunings are preferable to one heavy pruning each year. As a rule, do not attempt to dramatically alter the natural form of a shrub; instead, choose a species that has a natural tendency to grow into the form desired. Study the sizes and forms that various shrubs have attained in existing landscapes around town and look at the photographs in Section 2.

For special effect, shrubs can be pruned into geometric shapes or to look like animal figures. This practice, known as *topiary*, has become popular in recent years. Like hedges (Figure 30a, b), topiary plants are high-maintenance attention grabbers and should be used sparingly in most low-maintenance landscapes. Small-leafed shrubs like boxwood, Florida privet, surinam cherry, natal-plum, dwarf yaupon holly, pyracantha and others can be trained to achieve specific forms. Consult Appendix 1 for a complete list of plants suitable for training into hedges and topiaries.

An *espaliered* plant is one that has been trained to grow more or less in a flat plane against a wall, fence, or trellis (Figure 31). This technique requires frequent pinching and pruning, and not all shrubs are adaptable to these measures. Pyracantha, camellia, burford holly and natal-plum make excellent espalier plants (Figure 32).

Large shrubs (e.g., cocoplum, photinia, ligustrum, wax-myrtle and pittosporum) can be trained into small trees by gradually

Figure 31. Golden dewdrop espaliered on a wooden trellis.

removing all the foliage and small branches from the lower portion of the stem(s). The removal process should take 1 to 3 years to complete and should not start before a plant is about 8 feet tall. By allowing the plant to reach this height, the main trunk has time to develop properly. Leaving small branches along the lower trunk during this period will create a stronger trunk and a sturdier tree. The

longer the small branches remain on the trunk, the thicker and stronger the trunk becomes.

When to prune

Shrubs in hardiness zones 10 and 11 are pruned year-round. However, shrubs that are heavily pruned in fall or winter begin actively producing new growth and, therefore, could be severely damaged by unusually cold weather. Shrubs can be lightly pruned anytime with little increase in cold damage. Early pruning on young shrubs encourages branching and fullness, which are frequently desirable characteristics of landscape plants. Some shrubs set their flower buds on the previous season's growth and the buds winter over on this older growth (Table 4). For example, azaleas form flower buds in early summer for the following year's flower display. Therefore, prune spring-flowering shrubs such as azaleas and spireas in late spring before the flower buds set for the next season. Additional pruning or pinching

Figure 32. Pyracantha, southern magnolia and other plants can be trained against a wall as espaliers.

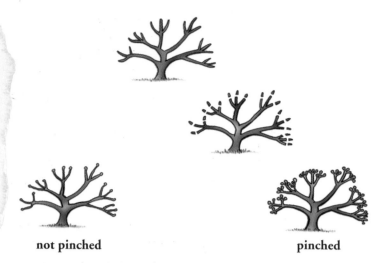

not pinched   pinched

Figure 33. Pinching encourages lateral shoot development and more flower buds.

Shrubs that produce flowers on the current season's new growth (e.g., abelia, hibiscus, rose) are usually pruned while dormant (Table 9). Developing shoots also can be pinched to encourage lateral branching, which in turn will create more flowers. Moderate to severe pruning may encourage production of fewer but larger blossoms or blossom clusters on some species.

during the interval between the end of the flower display and early summer will not reduce the number of flower buds set. Pinching back the new shoots on azaleas anytime from several weeks after shoots begin elongating through the early summer will encourage them to branch laterally. Each of these lateral branches is likely to develop a flower bud. For this reason, a pinched plant will produce many more flowers the following year than will an unpinched plant (Figure 33). Pruning between July and the beginning of the flower display will remove flower buds and reduce next year's flower display, but should not affect the health of the plant.

Closure (callusing) of pruning wounds on most shrubs will be most rapid if pruning is conducted just before or immediately following the spring growth flush. A closed wound is not only more aesthetically pleasing, but it also discourages insects, diseases and decay organisms from entering the plant.

Most evergreens, such as podocarpus, holly, boxwood, ligustrum, juniper and wax-myrtle, can be pruned anytime. To encourage rapid shoot development and the greatest overall plant growth, prune just prior to bud swell in the spring. To retard growth for

---

Table 8. Winter- and spring-flowering shrubs that can be pruned after flowering but before flower buds form for next year's bloom.*

azaleas	spireas
some hydrangea	Indian hawthorn
banana shrub	star and saucer magnolia
camellia	

* The only effect from pruning at other times is a reduction in the number of flower buds.

Table 9. Shrubs that can be pruned during the dormant season. (Flowers are produced on current season's growth.)

allamanda	plumbago
abelia	thryallis
hibiscus	golden dewdrop
oleander	bougainvillea
rose	princess-flower
crape myrtle	

Figure 34. *Removing the tips of branches with thumb and forefinger is called "pinching."*

Pruning techniques

Shrubs are pruned either by "heading" or by "thinning." Heading is the cutting of twigs or young branches back to a bud or node. When heading is done using the thumb and forefinger to remove the tips of branches it is referred to as "pinching" (Figure 34). Usually an increased number of shoots and leaves results from heading, producing denser growth at the outer edge of the canopy of the plant. New growth is typically vigorous and upright, with two to several buds developing into shoots just behind the cut (Figure 35). If properly applied to shrubs, pleasing forms can be created and maintained. New growth may be so thick that it shades lower and interior foliage, forming a top-heavy plant with few or no leaves on the inside of the plant. To avoid this problem, head the shrub's shoots to several different lengths (Figure 36). When heading, make the cut

maximum dwarfing effect, prune just after each growth flush, when leaves have expanded fully. Late summer pruning may stimulate an additional flush of shoot growth. These shoots could be damaged by an early frost.

Cold injury can be minimized if pruning is conducted close to the spring bud break. Late fall and early winter pruning can stimulate new growth, particularly during a mild period of the winter. The succulent stems that are produced as a consequence are not cold hardy and can be easily damaged, even by a light frost. Even if growth is not stimulated by pruning, low winter temperatures can cause cambium damage. This is particularly true of shrubs that are marginally hardy. If in doubt about cold susceptibility, it is best to delay heavy pruning until just before growth begins in the spring.

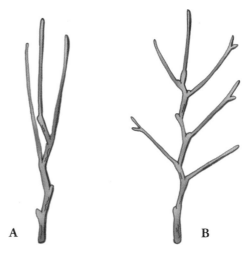

A   B

Figure 35. *(A) Growth from a shoot that has been headed. (B) Growth from an unpruned shoot.*

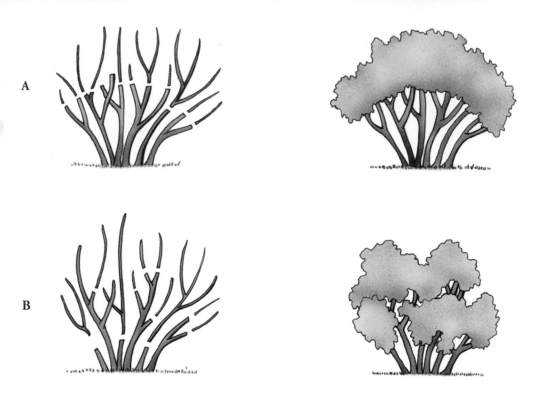

A

B

Figure 36. *(A) Shrub with all shoots headed back to the same height develops new foliage mainly toward the top of the plant. (B) Shrub remains fuller when shoots are headed to different heights.*

at a slight slant 1/8 to 1/4 inch above a healthy bud (Figure 37). The bud should be facing the direction preferred for new growth.

Thinning (Figure 39) is the removal of branches back to the trunk or to the ground. A thinned shrub usually remains about the same size after pruning. Reducing the height of a trunk or stem by cutting back to an existing lateral branch is referred to as drop-crotching. (Some horticulturists refer to this as thinning; others call it heading.) Depending on whether the shrub is thinned or drop-crotched, a shrub can take on a more open appearance or new growth can be encouraged inside the crown. If thinning is heavy (i.e., more than one-third of foliage is removed), sprouts will

form along stems. If the shrub is lightly thinned, sprouts are not likely to develop. Shrubs are thinned primarily to reduce plant density while maintaining a natural appearance. This technique differs from hedging or heading to the same spot on all branches, which will give a shrub a formal, controlled appearance.

A properly pruned shrub is a work of art and beauty and does not look as if it has been pruned. Pruning cuts should not be visible but located inside the plant where they will be covered by remaining foliage (Figure 38). Cuts can also be positioned so the cut surface faces the back of the shrub.

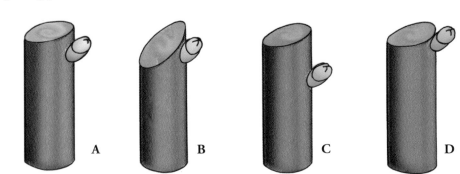

A   B   C   D

Figure 37. *(A) Proper location and angle of pruning cut. (B) Too slanted. (C) Too far from the bud. (D) Too close to the bud.*

Figure 38. Cut back excessively long branches to a lateral branch or bud.

The first step in pruning a shrub is to remove all dead, diseased or injured branches. Remove branches that cross or touch each other and those that look out of place. If the shrub is still too dense or large, remove some of the oldest branches. Cut back excessively long branches to a lateral branch (Figure 38) or bud that is 6 to 12 inches below the desirable plant height (Figure 36). Thinning (Figure 39) also may be desirable. Do not use hedge shears. Cut each branch separately to different lengths with hand pruners. This will maintain a neat informal shrub with a natural shape. (Plants sheared into hard geometric shapes look out of place in a landscape designed to look natural.) For a discussion of formal pruning, see the segment to follow on hedge pruning.

Rejuvenation of Shrubs

Rejuvenation is a drastic method of pruning old shrubs that have become much too large or have a large amount of non-flowering wood. The best time for rejuvenation is in late winter or early spring, just before growth begins. Large, old shrubs should not be rejuvenated during late summer. Except in hardiness zones 10 and 11, new growth will be stimulated and possibly killed by cold weather in the winter.

Before pruning

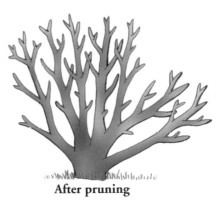

After pruning

Figure 39. Correctly thinned shrub remains about the same height as before pruning. Secondary branches are removed all along the main stems, especially toward the ends.

Multiple stem shrubs are rejuvenated by cutting back all stems at ground level over a period of 12 to 18 months. At the first pruning, remove one-third of the old, mature stems (Figure 40). Six months later, take out one-half of the remaining old stems and head back long shoots growing from the previous pruning cuts. At the

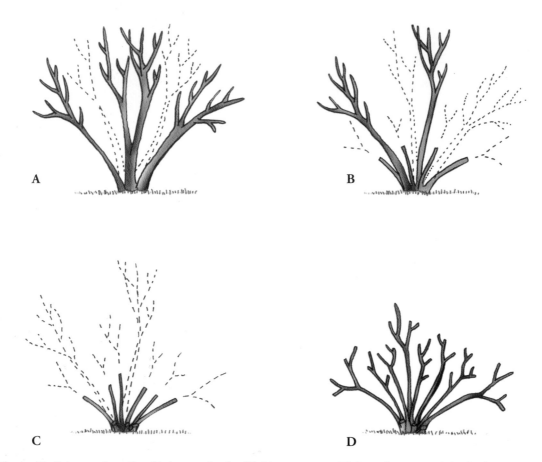

Figure 40. *Rejuvenation of multiple stem shrubs. (A) First pruning. (B) Second pruning. (C) Third pruning. (D) Rejuvenated shrub.*

third pruning 6 months later, remove the remaining old wood and head back the long new shoots.

Rejuvenating cane-type shrubs, such as nandina and mahonia, is best done on a 2- or 3-year cycle. The tallest canes are pruned to stubs 3 to 6 inches above the soil line

Figure 41. *Instead of clipping a hedge only along the outside of the canopy as in Figure 20a, consider making heading cuts back inside the hedge and leaving many shorter branches uncut. This results in a softer effect.*

during the first spring, just as growth begins. By the second spring, last year's medium-sized canes have grown to become tall canes and should be cut back to 3-inch stubs. Canes from the first year's pruning have already begun to grow and are 1 to 3 feet tall by now. In the third spring, the canes that were the shortest in the first spring are now fairly tall and can be cut back. In this way, there is always foliage near the ground and the shrubs can be kept from becoming leggy. After nandina canes are cut, they generally will not flower during the growing season that follows their pruning.

Hedge Pruning

The method you choose for hedge pruning will be determined by the type of hedge you want. An informal hedge is maintained by making heading and drop-

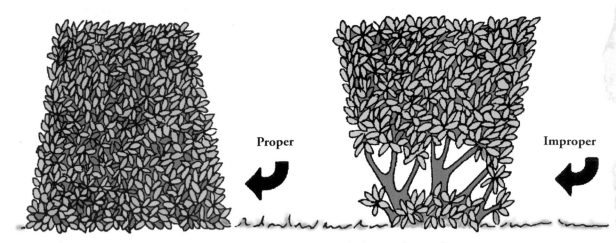

Proper   **Improper**

Figure 42. Shrubs pruned as a solid hedge should be wider at the bottom than at the top.

crotch cuts only on the longest shoots, 6 to 12 inches back inside the outer edge of the hedge. The shorter shoots remain intact and form the outside edge of the now smaller hedge. The outer edge of the canopy appears more open and softer than a clipped formal hedge (Figure 41).

Figure 43. Results of improper pruning. To avoid this, train the hedge so it is narrower at the top than at the bottom.

The desired appearance of a formal hedge is a sharply defined geometric shape (Figure 30a). A square or box shape is most common. There are two important factors to remember when pruning formal hedges: 1) hedges should be clipped while new growth is green and succulent; 2) plants should be trimmed so the base of the hedge is wider than the top (Figure 42). Hedges pruned with a narrow base will lose lower leaves and branches shaded by the top (Figure 43). This condition will worsen with age, resulting in sparse growth at ground level and an unattractive hedge that does not give desired privacy. Flowering hedges grown formally should be sheared only after they have flowered to prevent reduction in the number of subsequent blooms. If the blooms are of secondary importance, pruning may be conducted at any time.

Wrap-Up

Now you're ready to transform your landscape like a professional. Section 1 of this book provided you with a solid foundation on which to build, maintain, or renovate your landscape. You've noted the light and drainage conditions around your yard, and you've had your soil pH tested. You have determined the size of shrub (at maturity) that you want for each area of the yard. Using Section 2, you selected shrubs that will flourish in your yard by matching the attributes of the shrubs with your landscape conditions. Section 3 guided you through planting shrubs and also will help you care for your shrubs for years to come. Enjoy creating a new, low-maintenance landscape that will add beauty and value to your home.

Appendix 1. Shrubs suited for hedging.

Anise	Fiddlewood	Sandankwa Viburnum
Balfour Aralia	Firebush	Scaevola
Barbados Cherry	Florida Anise	'Schilling's Dwarf' Holly
Bay-Cedar	Florida Boxwood	Seven-Year Apple
Bougainvillea	Florida Privet	Silverthorn
Boxthorn	Fraser Photinia	Simpson's Stopper
Brush Cherry	Gardenia	Snowbush
Bush Clock Vine	Golden Dewdrop	Southern Waxmyrtle
Buttonwood	Indian Hawthorn	Spanish Stopper
Cape Honeysuckle	Ixora	Spicewood
Chenille Plant	Japanese Barberry	Surinam Cherry
Chinese Hat Plant	Japanese Holly	Sweet Osmanthus
Cleyera	Japanese Pittosporum	Sweet Viburnum
Cocoplum	Japanese Privet	Texas Sage
Compact Burford Holly	Laurestinus Viburnum	Thryallis
Copperleaf	Littleleaf Boxwood	Tropical Hibiscus
Crape-Jasmine	Marlberry	Turk's Cap
Croton	Orange-Jasmine	Variegated Chinese Privet
Downy Jasmine	Pentas	Variegated Pittosporum
Dwarf Fothergilla	Plumbago	Varnish-Leaf
Dwarf Oleander	Powderpuff	Wild-Coffee
Dwarf Red Powderpuff	Princess-Flower	Winter Cinnamon
Dwarf Schefflera	Red Bottlebrush	Wintergreen Barberry
False Heather	Red Stopper	Yew Podocarpus

Appendix 2. Shrubs tolerant of wet soil.

African Iris*	Firethorn	Selloum
Balfour Aralia	Florida Gamma Grass	Silverthorn
Bigleaf Hydrangea	Florida Privet*	Simpson's Stopper
Bird-of-Paradise	Gallberry*	Southern Waxmyrtle*
Butterfly-Bush	Giant Spider-Lily*	Spicewood
Butterfly Ginger	Hair Awn Muhly Grass	String-Lily*
Buttonwood*	Leather Fern	Sweetshrub
Caricature Plant	Marsh Grass*	Turk's Cap
Copperleaf	Oak-Leaf Hydrangea	Umbrella Sedge*
Dog-Hobble*	Rose-of-Sharon	Variegated Shellflower
Dracaena	Royal Fern*	Weeping Fig
Fakahatchee Grass	Sandankwa Viburnum	
Firebush	'Schilling's Dwarf' Holly	*Especially tolerant of flooding*

Appendix 3. Shrubs tolerant of drought.

Adam's Needle
'Allspice' Banana Shrub
American Beautyberry
Anise
Arborvitae
Balfour Aralia
Banana Shrub
Bay-Cedar
'Blue Vase' Juniper
Bougainvillea
Boxthorn
Bush Clock Vine
Buttonwood
Cape Honeysuckle
Cardboard Plant
Century Plant
Chenille Plant
Chinese Fountain Grass
Chinese Hat Plant
Cleyera
Cocoplum
Common Camellia
Compact Burford Holly
Coontie
Crape-Jasmine
Dog-Hobble
Downy Jasmine
Dracaena
Dwarf Chinese Holly
Dwarf Natal-Plum
Dwarf Oleander
Dwarf Poinciana
Dwarf Red Powderpuff
Dwarf Schefflera
European Fan Palm
Fakahatchee Grass
False Heather
Fiddlewood
Firebush
Firecracker Plant

Firethorn
Florida Boxwood
Florida Gamma Grass
Florida Privet
Florida Tetrazygia
Fortune's Mahonia
Fraser Photinia
Gallberry
Giant Spider-Lily
Glossy Abelia
Golden Dewdrop
Hair Awn Muhly Grass
Indian Hawthorn
Inkberry
   (*Scaevola plumieri*)
Ixora
Jamaican Caper
Japanese Barberry
Japanese Holly
Japanese Pittosporum
Japanese Privet
King Sago
Lady Palm
Laurestinus Viburnum
Littleleaf Boxwood
Marlberry
Marsh Grass
Nandina
Necklace-Pod
Needle Palm
Oleander
Orange-Jasmine
Pampas Grass
Peregrina
Plumbago
Powderpuff
Prickly-Pear Cactus
Queen Sago
Red Bottlebrush
Red-Edged Dracaena

Red Stopper
Reeve's Spiraea
Rose-of-Sharon
Round-Leaf Hawthorn
Sandankwa Viburnum
Saw Palmetto
Scaevola
'Schilling's Dwarf'
   Holly
Sea-Lavender
Senna
Seven-Year Apple
Silverthorn
Simpson's Stopper
Snake Plant
Snowbush
Spanish Bayonet
Spanish Dagger
Spanish Stopper
Spicewood
Surinam Cherry
Sweet Osmanthus
Sweet Viburnum
Sweetshrub
Tender Fountain Grass
Texas Sage
'Torulosa' Juniper
Turk's Cap
Variegated Caribbean
   Agave
Variegated Chinese
   Privet
Variegated Pittosporum
Varnish-Leaf
Weeping Fig
Wild-Coffee
Winter Cinnamon
Wintergreen Barberry
Yesterday-Today-and-
   Tomorrow
Yew Podocarpus

Adam's Needle
African Bush-Daisy
African Iris
Angel's Trumpet-Tree
Bigleaf Hydrangea
Bird-of-Paradise
Bougainvillea
Bush Allamanda
Bush Clock Vine
Butterfly-Bush
Butterfly Ginger
Candle Bush
Cape Honeysuckle
Caricature Plant
Cassia
Century Plant
Chaste Tree
Chenille Plant
Chinese Fountain Grass
Chinese Hat Plant
Cigar Plant
Common Camellia
Crape-Jasmine
Downy Jasmine
Dwarf Fothergilla
Dwarf Natal-Plum
Dwarf Oleander
Dwarf Poinciana
Dwarf Red Powderpuff
False Heather
'Fashion' Azalea

Fatsia
Fiddlewood
Firebush
Firecracker Plant
Firethorn
Florida Anise
Fraser Photinia
Gardenia
'George Taber' Azalea
Giant Spider-Lily
Glossy Abelia
Golden Dewdrop
Golden Shrimp Plant
Hair Awn Muhly Grass
Heliconia
Indian Hawthorn
Ixora
Jacobinia
Jamaican Caper
Japanese Privet
Laurestinus Viburnum
Marlberry
Marsh Grass
Nandina
Necklace-Pod
Oak-Leaf Hydrangea
Oleander
Orange-Jasmine
Pampas Grass
Pentas
Peregrina

Pink Pinxter Azalea
Plumbago
Powderpuff
Prickly-Pear Cactus
Princess-Flower
Red Bottlebrush
Reeve's Spiraea
Rose-of-Sharon
Round-Leaf Hawthorn
Sanchezia
Senna
Shrimp Plant
Snowbush
Spanish Bayonet
Spanish Dagger
Star Magnolia
String-Lily
Sweet Viburnum
Sweetshrub
Tender Fountain Grass
Texas Sage
Thryallis
Tropical Hibiscus
Tropical Snowball
Turk's Cap
Variegated Shellflower
Winter Cinnamon
Wintergreen Barberry
Yellow-Alder
Yellow-Elder
Yesterday-Today-and-Tomorrow

Appendix 5. Shrubs less than 6 feet tall.

African Bush-Daisy
African Iris
Bird-of-Paradise
Bougainvillea*
Bush Allamanda
Bush Clock Vine
Butterfly Ginger
Cape Honeysuckle
Cardboard Plant
Chenille Plant
Chinese Fountain Grass
Cigar Plant
Coontie
Dog-Hobble
Downy Jasmine
Dwarf Fothergilla
Dwarf Natal-Plum

Dwarf Oleander
Dwarf Red Powderpuff
Fakahatchee Grass
False Heather
'Fashion' Azalea
Firecracker Plant
Florida Gamma Grass
Fortune's Mahonia
Giant Spider-Lily
Golden Shrimp Plant
Hair Awn Muhly Grass
Holly Fern
Inkberry
   (*Scaevola plumieri*)
Jacobinia
Littleleaf Boxwood

Marsh Grass
Pentas
Persian Shield
Royal Fern
Sanchezia
Sea-Lavender
Shrimp Plant
Snake Plant
String-Lily
Tender Fountain Grass
Variegated Caribbean
   Agave
Wintergreen Barberry
Yellow-Alder

Dwarf cultivars are available

Appendix 6. Shrubs native to Florida.

Adam's Needle
American Beautyberry
Anise
Bay-Cedar
Buttonwood
Cocoplum
Coontie
Dog-Hobble
Fakahatchee Grass
Fiddlewood
Firebush
Florida Anise
Florida Boxwood
Florida Gamma Grass
Florida Privet
Florida Tetrazygia
Gallberry
Golden Dewdrop
Hair Awn Muhly Grass

Inkberry
   (*Scaevola plumieri*)
Jamaican Caper
Leather Fern
Marlberry
Marsh Grass
Necklace-Pod
Needle Palm
Oak-Leaf Hydrangea
Pink Pinxter Azalea
Prickly-Pear Cactus
Red Stopper
Saw Palmetto
Sea-Lavender
Seven-Year Apple
Simpson's Stopper
Southern Waxmyrtle
Spanish Bayonet
Spanish Dagger

Spanish Stopper
Spicewood
String-Lily
Sweetshrub
Varnish-Leaf
Wild-Coffee
Winter Cinnamon
Yaupon Holly

A

abelia 26, 98
Abelia x *grandiflora* 26
Abelia, Glossy (*Abelia* x *grandiflora*) 26
Acalypha hispida 26
Acalypha wilkesiana 26
Acrostichum daneiifolium 27
Adam's Needle (*Yucca filamentosa*) 82, 105, 106, 107
African Bush-Daisy (*Gamolepis chrysanthemoides*) 47, 106, 107
African Iris (*Dietes vegeta*) 6, 42, 104, 106, 107
Agave americana 27
Agave angustifolia 'Marginata' 27
Agave, Variegated Caribbean
    (*Agave angustifolia* 'Marginata') 27
air drainage 14
Alder, Yellow- (*Turnera ulmifolia*) 79
Allamanda neriifolia 28
Allamanda, Bush (*Allamanda neriifolia*) 28, 98
Allspice, Carolina (*Calycanthus floridus*) 33
'Allspice' Banana Shrub
    (*Michelia doltsopa* x *figo* 'Allspice') 59, 105
Aloe Yucca (*Yucca aloifolia*) 81
Alpinia zerumbet 'Variegata' 28
Althea, Shrub- (*Hibiscus syriacus*) 50
American Beautyberry (*Callicarpa americana*) 33, 105, 107
Andorra Juniper 7
Angel's Trumpet-Tree (*Brugmansia* spp.) 30, 106
Anise (*Illicium parviflorum*) 8, 9, 53, 104, 105, 107
Anise, Florida (*Illicium floridanum*) 53
Anise, Purple (*Illicium floridanum*) 53
Anise, Small (*Illicium parviflorum*) 53
aphids 96
Apple, Seven-Year (*Casasia clusiifolia*) 35, 104, 105, 107
Aralia, Balfour (*Polyscias pinnata*) 67, 104, 105
Arborvitae (*Platycladus orientalis*) 66, 105
Ardisia escallonioides 28
Aucuba (*Aucuba japonica*) 29
Aucuba japonica 29
Aucuba, Japanese (*Aucuba japonica*) 29
automatic rain switch 87
azalea 7, 97-98, 106, 107
Azalea, Pink Pinxter (*Rhododendron canescens*) 70, 106, 107
Azalea, 'Fashion' (*Rhododendron* 'Fashion') 70, 106, 107
Azalea, Formosa 7
Azalea, 'George Taber'
    (*Rhododendron* 'George Taber') 70, 106
Azalea (dwarf), Kurume 9

B

Balfour Aralia (*Polyscias pinnata*) 67, 104, 105
balled and burlapped 19, 20, 21

Bamboo, Heavenly (*Nandina domestica*) 62
Bamboo Palm, Hardy (*Chamaedorea microspadix*) 36
Banana Shrub (*Michelia figo*) 60, 98, 105
Banana Shrub, 'Allspice'
    (*Michelia doltsopa* x *figo* 'Allspice') 59, 105
Barbados Cherry (*Malpighia glabra*) 59, 104
Barbados Flowerfence (*Caesalpinia pulcherrima*) 32
Barberry, Japanese (*Berberis thunbergii*) 29, 104, 105
Barberry, Wintergreen (*Berberis julianae*) 29, 104, 105, 106, 107
Bay-Cedar (*Suriana maritima*) 76, 104, 105, 107
Bayberry, Southern (*Myrica cerifera*) 61
Beach Naupaka (*Scaevola frutescens*) 72
Beautyberry, American (*Callicarpa americana*) 33, 105, 107
bed design 12-14
Berberis julianae 29
Berberis thunbergii 29
Bird-of-Paradise (*Strelitzia reginae*) 6, 75, 104, 106, 107
Blackhaw (*Viburnum obovatum*) 80
Blue Rug Juniper 9
'Blue Vase' Juniper
    (*Juniperus chinensis* 'Blue Vase') 9, 55, 105
Boston Fern 8
Bottlebrush, Lemon (*Callistemon citrinus*) 33
Bottlebrush, Red (*Callistemon citrinus*) 33
Bougainvillea (*Bougainvillea* spp.) 30, 98, 104, 105, 106, 107
Bougainvillea spp. 30
Box, Littleleaf (*Buxus microphylla*) 31
Box-Leaf Eugenia (*Eugenia foetida*) 44
Boxthorn (*Severinia buxifolia*) 74, 104, 105
boxwood 31, 72, 96, 98
Boxwood, Florida (*Schaefferia frutescens*) 72
Boxwood, Littleleaf (*Buxus microphylla*) 31
Breynia disticha 30
Brugmansia spp. 30
Brunfelsia grandiflora 31
Brush Cherry (*Syzygium paniculatum*) 76, 104, 107
Buddleia spp. 31
Burford Holly, Compact
    (*Ilex cornuta* 'Burfordii Nana') 51, 97, 104, 105
Burford Holly, Dwarf
    (*Ilex cornuta* 'Burfordii Nana') 51, 97
burlap 19, 20, 21
    natural 21
    synthetic 21
Bush Allamanda (*Allamanda neriifolia*) 28, 98, 106, 107
Bush Clock Vine (*Thunbergia erecta*) 78, 104, 105, 106, 107
Bush-Daisy, African (*Gamolepis chrysanthemoides*) 47, 106, 107
Butterfly Ginger (*Hedychium coronarium*) 49, 104, 106, 107
Butterfly Iris (*Dietes vegeta*) 42

Butterfly-Bush (*Buddleia* spp.) 31, 104, 106

Buttonwood (*Conocarpus erectus* var. *seriacus*) 38, 104, 105, 107

Buttonwood, Silver 7

Buxus microphylla 31

C

Cactus, Prickly-Pear (*Opuntia* spp.) 63

Caesalpinia pulcherrima 32

Calliandra haematocephala 32

Calliandra haematocephala 'Nana' 32

Callicarpa americana 33

Callistemon citrinus 33

callusing 98

Calycanthus floridus 33

Calyptranthes pallens 34

cambium damage 99

camellia 7, 34, 97-98

Camellia japonica 34

Camellia, Common (*Camellia japonica*) 7, 34, 98, 105, 106

Candle Bush (*Cassia alata*) 36, 106

Canella winterana 34

Cape Honeysuckle (*Tecomaria capensis*) 77, 104, 105, 106, 107

Cape-Jasmine (*Gardenia jasminoides*) 48

Cape Plumbago (*Plumbago auriculata*) 67

Caper, Jamaican (*Capparis cynophallophora*) 35

Capparis cynophallophora 35

Cardboard Cycad (*Zamia furfuracea*) 7, 8, 83

Cardboard Plant (*Zamia furfuracea*) 83, 105, 107

Caricature Plant (*Graptophyllum pictum*) 48, 104, 106

Carissa macrocarpa 35

Carolina Allspice (*Calycanthus floridus*) 33

Casasia clusiifolia 35

Cassia (*Cassia bicapsularis*) 36, 106

Cassia alata 36

Cassia bicapsularis 36

Cassia, Desert- (*Senna polyphylla*) 73

Century Plant (*Agave americana*) 27, 105, 106

Chalcas (*Murraya paniculata*) 61

Chamaedorea microspadix 36

Chamaerops humilis 37

Chaste Tree (*Vitex agnus-castus*) 81, 106

Chenille Plant (*Acalypha hispida*) 26, 104, 105, 106, 107

Cherry, Barbados (*Malpighia glabra*) 59, 104

Cherry, Brush (*Syzygium paniculatum*) 76, 104, 107

Cherry, Surinam (*Eugenia uniflora*) 45, 96

Chinese Elm 7

Chinese Fountain Grass (*Pennisetum alopecuroides*) 64, 105, 106, 107

Chinese Hat Plant (*Holmskioldia sanguinea*) 50, 104, 105, 106

Chinese Hibiscus (*Hibiscus rosa-sinensis*) 50

Chinese Privet, Variegated (*Ligustrum sinense* 'Variegatum') 57

Chrysobalanus icaco 37

Cigar Flower (*Cuphea ignea*) 40

Cigar Plant (*Cuphea ignea*) 40, 106, 107

Cinnamon, Wild (*Canella winterana*) 34

Cinnamon, Winter (*Canella winterana*) 34

Citharexylum fruticosum 37

Cleyera (*Ternstroemia gymnanthera*) 77, 104, 105

climate 14-16

climatic sections 14-16

Clock Vine, Bush (*Thunbergia erecta*) 78, 104, 105, 106, 107

Coastal Leucothoe (*Leucothoe axillaris*) 57

Cocoplum (*Chrysobalanus icaco*) 37, 97, 104, 105, 107

Codiaeum variegatum 38

cold injury 14-15, 19, 99

Common Camellia (*Camellia japonica*) 7, 34, 105, 106

Compact Burford Holly (*Ilex cornuta* 'Burfordii Nana') 51, 97, 104, 105

compost 23

Conocarpus erectus var. *seriacus* 38

conservation
    energy 4
    water 4, 88-90

consumption
    energy 86
    water 86, 87

container-grown plants 19-20

Coontie (*Zamia floridana*) 8, 82, 105, 107

Cooperative Extension agent 92

Copperleaf (*Acalypha wilkesiana*) 26, 104

Cordyline terminalis 38

Cortaderia selloana 39

county Extension office 92

Crape Myrtle (*Lagerstroemia* spp.) 7, 9, 56, 98

Crape Myrtle, Queen's 8

Crape-Jasmine (*Tabernaemontana divaricata*) 76, 104, 105, 106

Crinum americanum 39

Crinum x *amabile* 39

Croton (*Codiaeum variegatum*) 38, 104

Cuphea hyssopifolia 40

Cuphea ignea 40

Cycad, Cardboard (*Zamia furfuracea*) 7, 8, 83

Cycas circinalis 40

Cycas revoluta 41

Cyperus alternifolius 41

Cyrtomium falcatum 41

D

Dahoon Holly 8

Daisy-Bush (*Gamolepis chrysanthemoides*) 47

decay organisms 98

deficiencies
    magnesium 93-94
    micronutrient 15, 90, 94

Desert-Cassia (*Senna polyphylla*) 73

Dewdrop, Golden (*Duranta repens*) 44, 97, 98

Dieffenbachia spp. 42

Dietes vegeta 42

disease 18, 95-96, 98
    leaf spot 19
Dodonaea viscosa 42
Dog-Hobble (*Leucothoe axillaris*) 57, 104, 105, 107
Dombeya spp. 43
dormancy 15
Downy Jasmine (*Jasminum multiflorum*) 54, 104, 105, 106, 107
Dracaena (*Dracaena deremensis*) 43, 104, 105
Dracaena deremensis 43
Dracaena marginata 43
Dracaena, Red-Edged (*Dracaena marginata*) 43
Dragon-Tree, Madagascar (*Dracaena marginata*) 43
drip emitters 88-89
drip line 22, 92
drop-crotching 99-100, 102
drought 25, 85, 105
drought stress 87
Dumbcane, Giant (*Dieffenbachia* spp.) 42
Duranta repens 44
Dwarf Burford Holly (*Ilex cornuta* 'Burfordii Nana') 51
Dwarf Chinese Holly (*Ilex cornuta* 'Rotunda') 52
Dwarf Fakahatchee Grass (*Tripsacum dactyloides*) 79
Dwarf Fothergilla (*Fothergilla gardenii*) 47, 104, 106, 107
Dwarf Gamma Grass 9
Dwarf Kurume Azalea 9
Dwarf Natal-Plum (*Carissa macrocarpa*) 7, 35, 105, 106, 107
Dwarf Oleander
    (*Nerium oleander* 'Petite Pink') 62, 104, 105, 106, 107
Dwarf Pittosporum 9
Dwarf Poinciana (*Caesalpinia pulcherrima*) 32, 105, 106
Dwarf Procumbens Juniper 8
Dwarf Red Powderpuff (*Calliandra haematocephala* 'Nana') 32, 104, 105, 106, 107
Dwarf Schefflera (*Schefflera arboricola*) 73, 104, 105
Dwarf Yaupon Holly (*Ilex vomitoria* 'Schilling's Dwarf') 7, 53, 96

E

East Palatka Holly 8
Eastern Gamma Grass (*Tripsacum dactyloides*) 79
Elaeagnus pungens 44
Elaeagnus, Thorny (*Elaeagnus pungens*) 44
Elder, Yellow- (*Tecoma stans*) 77, 106
Elm, Chinese 7
espalier plants 97
Eugenia, Box-Leaf (*Eugenia foetida*) 44
Eugenia foetida 44
Eugenia rhombea 45
Eugenia uniflora 45
European Fan Palm (*Chamaerops humilis*) 37, 105
'Evergreen Giant' Liriope 7

F

Fakahatchee Grass (*Tripsacum dactyloides*) 79, 104, 105, 107

Fakahatchee Grass, Dwarf
    (*Tripsacum floridana*) 79
False Heather (*Cuphea hyssopifolia*) 40, 104, 105, 106, 107
fan-jets 89
'Fashion' Azalea (*Rhododendron* 'Fashion') 70, 106, 107
Fatsia (*Fatsia japonica*) 45, 106
Fatsia japonica 45
Feijoa sellowiana 46
Fern, Holly (*Cyrtomium falcatum*) 41
Fern, Japanese Holly (*Cyrtomium falcatum*) 41
Fern, Leather (*Acrostichum daneifolium*) 8, 27
Fern, Royal (*Osmunda regalis*) 63
fertilization 90-95
fertilizer 90-95
    slow-release 85, 93-94
    water-soluble 93-94
    weed-and-feed 93
Ficus benjamina 46
Fiddlewood (*Citharexylum fruticosum*) 37, 104, 105, 106, 107
Fig, Weeping (*Ficus benjamina*) 46
Filamentose Yucca (*Yucca filamentosa*) 82
Firebush (*Hamelia patens*) 14, 49
Firecracker Plant (*Russelia equisetiformis*) 71, 105, 106, 107
Firethorn (*Pyracantha coccinea*) 68, 104, 105, 106
Flamingo Plant (*Justicia carnea*) 56
Florida Anise (*Illicium floridanum*) 53, 104, 106, 107
Florida Boxwood (*Schaefferia frutescens*) 72, 104, 105, 107
Florida Gamma Grass (*Tripsacum floridana*) 79, 104, 105, 107
Florida-Honeysuckle
    (*Rhododendron canescens*) 70
Florida native 16, 26-83. *See also* native plant
Florida Privet (*Forestiera segregata*) 46, 96, 104, 105, 107
Florida Tetrazygia (*Tetrazygia bicolor*) 78, 105, 107
Flowerfence, Barbados
    (*Caesalpinia pulcherrima*) 32
foliar sprays 94
Forestiera segregata 46
formal hedge 103
Formosa Azalea 7
Fortune's Mahonia (*Mahonia fortunei*) 58, 105, 107
Fothergilla gardenii 47
Fothergilla, Dwarf (*Fothergilla gardenii*) 47
Fountain Grass (*Pennisetum setaceum*) 64
Fountain Grass, Chinese
    (*Pennisetum alopecuroides*) 64
Fountain Grass, Tender (*Pennisetum setaceum*) 64
Fragrant Osmanthus 9
Fraser Photinia (*Photinia* x *fraseri*) 65, 104, 105, 106
Fringe Tree 6
frost 14-15, 19, 98-99

G

Gallberry (*Ilex glabra*) 52, 104, 105, 107

Galphimia glauca 47

Gamma Grass (*Tripsacum dactyloides*) 79

Gamma Grass, Dwarf 9

Gamma Grass, Eastern (*Tripsacum dactyloides*) 79

Gamma Grass, Florida (*Tripsacum floridana*) 79

Gamolepis chrysanthemoides 47

Garden Hydrangea (*Hydrangea macrophylla*) 51

Gardenia (*Gardenia jasminoides*) 6, 7, 19, 48, 95, 104, 106

Gardenia jasminoides 48

'George Taber' Azalea
(*Rhododendron* 'George Taber') 70, 106

Giant Dumbcane (*Dieffenbachia* spp.) 42

Giant Spider-Lily (*Crinum* x *amabile*) 39, 104, 105, 106, 107

Ginger 7

Ginger, Butterfly (*Hedychium coronarium*) 49

Ginger, Variegated Shell
(*Alpinia zerumbet* 'Variegata') 28

Glossy Abelia (*Abelia* x *grandiflora*) 26, 105, 106

Golden Dewdrop (*Duranta repens*) 44, 98, 104, 105, 106, 107

Golden Shrimp Plant (*Pachystachys lutea*) 64, 106, 107

graft union 19

grafted plants 19

Graptophyllum pictum 48

Grass, Chinese Fountain
(*Pennisetum alopecuroides*) 64

Grass, Dwarf Fakahatchee (*Tripsacum floridana*) 79

Grass, Dwarf Gamma 9

Grass, Eastern Gamma (*Tripsacum dactyloides*) 79

Grass, Fakahatchee (*Tripsacum dactyloides*) 79

Grass, Florida Gamma (*Tripsacum floridana*) 79

Grass, Gamma (*Tripsacum dactyloides*) 79

Grass, Hair Awn Muhly
(*Muhlenbergia capillaris*) 60, 104, 105, 106, 107

Grass, Japanese Silver (*Miscanthus sinensis*) 60

Grass, Marsh (*Spartina bakeri*) 74

Grass, Pampas (*Cortaderia selloana*) 39

Grass, Tender Fountain (*Pennisetum setaceum*) 64

ground covers 4, 5, 7, 8, 9, 10, 11, 18, 95

Guaiacum officinale 48

Guaiacum spp. 48

gumbo-limbo 9

Guava, Pineapple (*Feijoa sellowiana*) 46

H

Hair Awn Muhly Grass
(*Muhlenbergia capillaris*) 60, 104, 105, 106, 107

Hamelia patens 49

hardiness zones 14-15, 24, 26-83

Hardy Bamboo Palm (*Chamaedorea microspadix*) 36

Hawthorn, Indian (*Raphiolepis indica*) 6, 7, 9, 19, 68, 98

Hawthorn, Round-Leaf (*Raphiolepis umbellata*) 9, 69

Hawthorn, Yedda (*Raphiolepis umbellata*) 69

heading 99-102

Heather, False (*Cuphea hyssopifolia*) 40

Heather, Mexican (*Cuphea hyssopifolia*) 40

Heavenly Bamboo (*Nandina domestica*) 62

hedge pruning 102-103

Hedychium coronarium 49

Heliconia (*Heliconia* spp.) 49, 106

Heliconia spp. 49

herbicide 93

hibiscus 6, 7, 50, 98

Hibiscus rosa-sinensis 50

Hibiscus syriacus 50

Hibiscus, Chinese (*Hibiscus rosa-sinensis*) 50

Hibiscus, Tropical (*Hibiscus rosa-sinensis*) 50

holly 6, 7, 51-53, 98

Holly, Compact Burford
(*Ilex cornuta* 'Burfordii Nana') 51

Holly, Dahoon 8

Holly, Dwarf Burford
(*Ilex cornuta* 'Burfordii Nana') 51

Holly, Dwarf Chinese
(*Ilex cornuta* 'Rotunda') 52

Holly, Dwarf Yaupon (*Ilex vomitoria* 'Schilling's Dwarf')
53

Holly, East Palatka 8

Holly, Japanese (*Ilex crenata*) 52

Holly Fern (*Cyrtomium falcatum*) 41

Holly Fern, Japanese (*Cyrtomium falcatum*) 41

Holmskioldia sanguinea 50

Honeysuckle, Cape (*Tecomaria capensis*) 77

Honeysuckle, Florida- (*Rhododendron canescens*) 70

Hydrangea, Garden (*Hydrangea macrophylla*) 51

Hydrangea macrophylla 51

Hydrangea, Oak-Leaf (*Hydrangea quercifolia*) 51

Hydrangea quercifolia 51

I

Ilex cornuta 'Burfordii Nana' 51

Ilex cornuta 'Rotunda' 52

Ilex crenata 52

Ilex glabra 52

Ilex vomitoria 53

Illicium floridanum 53

Illicium parviflorum 53

Indian Hawthorn (*Raphiolepis indica*) 6, 7, 9, 19, 68, 98, 104, 105, 106

injury
cold 19, 99
mechanical 19

Inkberry (*Ilex glabra*) 52

Inkberry (*Scaevola plumieri*) 72, 105, 107

inorganic material 23

insect problems 95, 98

insecticides 96

invasive plant 36, 45, 57, 62

invasive potential 25

Iris, African (*Dietes vegeta*) 6, 42

Iris, Butterfly (*Dietes vegeta*) 42

irrigation 21, 85-90

irrigation, overhead systems 86-87

Ixora (*Ixora coccinea*) 6, 7, 54, 104, 105, 106
Ixora coccinea 54

J

Jacobinia (*Justicia carnea*) 56, 106, 107
Jacob's Coat (*Acalypha wilkesiana*) 26
Jamaican Caper (*Capparis cynophallophora*) 35, 105, 106, 107
Japanese Aucuba (*Aucuba japonica*) 29
Japanese Barberry (*Berberis thunbergii*) 29, 104, 105
Japanese Holly (*Ilex crenata*) 52, 104, 105
Japanese Holly Fern (*Cyrtomium falcatum*) 41
Japanese Pittosporum (*Pittosporum tobira*) 66, 104, 105
Japanese Privet (*Ligustrum japonicum*) 57, 104, 105, 106
Japanese Silver Grass (*Miscanthus sinensis*) 60
Japanese Ternstroemia (*Ternstroemia gymnanthera*) 77
Japanese Yew (*Podocarpus macrophyllus*) 67
Jasmine, Cape- (*Gardenia jasminoides*) 48
Jasmine, Crape- (*Tabernaemontana divaricata*) 76
Jasmine, Downy (*Jasminum multiflorum*) 54
Jasmine, Orange- (*Murraya paniculata*) 61
Jasminum multiflorum 54
Jatropha integerrima 54
juniper 6, 7, 8, 9, 98
Juniper, Andorra 7
Juniper, Blue Rug 9
Juniper, 'Blue Vase' (*Juniperus chinensis* 'Blue Vase') 9, 55
Juniper, Dwarf Procumbens 8
Juniper, Parson's 6, 7
Juniper, 'Torulosa' (*Juniperus chinensis* 'Torulosa') 55
Juniperus chinensis 'Blue Vase' 55
Juniperus chinensis 'Torulosa' 55
Justicia brandegeana 55
Justicia carnea 56

K

King Sago (*Cycas revoluta*) 41, 105
King's Mantle (*Thunbergia erecta*) 78
Kurume Azalea (Dwarf) 9

L

lacebugs 18
Lady Palm (*Rhapis excelsa*) 9, 69, 105
Lagerstroemia spp. 56
landscape
    designing 4-13
    site 4, 15
lantana 8
Laurestinus Viburnum (*Viburnum tinus*) 81, 104, 105, 106
leaf margins or tips, browning of 87
Leather Fern (*Acrostichum daneifolium*) 8, 27, 104, 107
Lemon Bottlebrush (*Callistemon citrinus*) 33
Leucophyllum frutescens 56
Leucothoe axillaris 57
Leucothoe, Coastal (*Leucothoe axillaris*) 57

Lidflower, Pale (*Calyptranthes pallens*) 34
light level 15
light requirement 26-83
Lignum Vitae (*Guaiacum officinale*) 48
Lignum Vitae (*Guaiacum* spp.) 48
ligustrum 10, 57, 97-98
Ligustrum japonicum 57
Ligustrum sinense 'Variegatum' 57
Lily, String- (*Crinum americanum*) 39
Lily, Swamp- (*Crinum americanum*) 39
Littleleaf Box (*Buxus microphylla*) 31
Littleleaf Boxwood (*Buxus microphylla*) 31, 104, 105, 107
Live Oak 7
Loblolly Bay 8

M

Madagascar Dragon-Tree (*Dracaena marginata*) 43
magnesium 93, 94
Magnolia kobus var. *stellata* 58
Magnolia, Southern 8, 97
Magnolia, Star (*Magnolia kobus* var. *stellata*) 58
Magnolia, Star and Saucer 98
mahogany 7
mahonia 58, 101
Mahonia fortunei 58
Mahonia, Fortune's (*Mahonia fortunei*) 58
Mallotonia gnaphalodes 58
Mallow, Wax (*Malvaviscus arboreus*) 59
Malpighia glabra 59
Malvaviscus arboreus 59
manganese 90, 95
Marlberry (*Ardisia escallonioides*) 28, 104, 105, 106, 107
Marsh Grass (*Spartina bakeri*) 74, 104, 105, 106, 107
mature size 4, 6, 25, 26-83
Mexican Heather (*Cuphea hyssopifolia*) 40
Michelia doltsopa x *figo* 'Allspice' 59
Michelia figo 60
microirrigation 88, 90
micronutrient deficiencies 94
Microspadix Palm (*Chamaedorea microspadix*) 36
microsprayers 89
microsprinklers 89
Miscanthus sinensis cultivars 60
Mother-in-Law's Tongue (*Sansevieria trifasciata*) 71
Mound-Lily Yucca (*Yucca gloriosa*) 82
Muhlenbergia capillaris 60
Muhly Grass, Hair Awn (*Muhlenbergia capillaris*) 60, 104, 105, 106, 107
mulches 22-23, 95
mulching 23
Murraya paniculata 61
Myrcianthes fragrans 61
Myrica cerifera 61

N

Nagi Podocarpus 7

Nandina (*Nandina domestica*) 7, 62, 101-102, 105, 106

Nandina domestica 62

natal-plum 7, 35, 96-97

Natal-Plum, Dwarf (*Carissa macrocarpa*) 7, 35

native plant/shrub 16, 17, 25, 26-83, 107

Naupaka, Beach (*Scaevola frutescens*) 72

Necklace-Pod (*Sophora tomentosa*) 74, 105, 106, 107

Needle Palm (*Rhapidophyllum hystrix*) 69, 105, 107

Nerium oleander 62

Nerium oleander 'Petite Pink' 62

nitrogen 92-93

nylon twine 21

O

Oak-Leaf Hydrangea (*Hydrangea quercifolia*) 51, 104, 106, 107

Oleander (*Nerium oleander*) 62, 98, 105, 106

Oleander, Dwarf (*Nerium oleander* 'Petite Pink') 62

Oleander, 'Petite Pink'
   (*Nerium oleander* 'Petite Pink') 62

Olive, Tea- (*Osmanthus fragrans*) 63

Opuntia spp. 63

Orange-Jasmine (*Murraya paniculata*) 61, 104, 105, 106

Orchid-tree 6

organic matter 22-23

Osmanthus fragrans 63

Osmanthus, Fragrant 9

Osmanthus, Sweet (*Osmanthus fragrans*) 63

Osmunda regalis 63

oxygen 94

P

Pachystachys lutea 64

Pale Lidflower (*Calyptranthes pallens*) 34

Palm, European Fan (*Chamaerops humilis*) 37

Palm, Hardy Bamboo (*Chamaedorea microspadix*) 36

Palm, Lady (*Rhapis excelsa*) 9, 69

Palm, Microspadix (*Chamaedorea microspadix*) 36

Palm, Needle (*Rhapidophyllum hystrix*) 69

Palm, Pindo 6

Palm, Yellow Butterfly 7

Palmetto, Saw (*Serenoa repens*) 6, 73

Pampas Grass (*Cortaderia selloana*) 39, 105, 106

Parson's Juniper 6, 7

peat 23

Pennisetum, Chinese (*Pennisetum alopecuroides*) 64

Pennisetum alopecuroides 64

Pennisetum setaceum 64

Pentas (*Pentas lanceolata*) 65, 104, 106, 107

Pentas lanceolata 65

Peregrina (*Jatropha integerrima*) 54, 105, 106

Persian Shield (*Strobilanthes dyeranus*) 75, 107

pests 18-19, 96

'Petite Pink' Oleander
   (*Nerium oleander* 'Petite Pink') 62

Philodendron selloum 65

phosphate 92, 93. *See also* phosphoric acid

phosphoric acid 93. *See also* phosphorous

phosphorous 91, 93. *See also* phosphoric acid

photinia 65, 97

Photinia x *fraseri* 65

Photinia, Fraser (*Photinia* x *fraseri*) 65

Photinia, Red-Tip 4, 19

pinching 97-99

Pindo Palm 6

pineapple 9

Pineapple Guava (*Feijoa sellowiana*) 46

Pink Pinxter Azalea (*Rhododendron canescens*) 70, 106, 107

Pinwheel Flower (*Tabernaemontana divaricata*) 6, 76

Pitchapple 9

pittosporum 4, 66, 97

Pittosporum, Dwarf 9

Pittosporum tobira 66

Pittosporum tobira 'Variegata' 66

Pittosporum, Japanese (*Pittosporum tobira*) 66

Pittosporum, Variegated
   (*Pittosporum tobira* 'Variegata') 66

plant
   architecture 17
   canopy 19, 85
   form 17
   shape 95, 96, 103

planting
   density 18
   hole 16, 21-22

Platycladus orientalis 66

Plumbago (*Plumbago auriculata*) 7, 67, 98, 104, 105, 106

Plumbago auriculata 67

Plumbago, Cape (*Plumbago auriculata*) 67

podocarpus 7

Podocarpus, Nagi 7

Podocarpus, Yew (*Podocarpus macrophyllus*) 7, 67, 98

Podocarpus macrophyllus 67

Poinciana, Dwarf (*Caesalpinia pulcherrima*) 32

Poinciana, Yellow 6

Polyscias pinnata 67

potash 92, 93. *See also* potassium

potassium 91, 93-94. *See also* potash

potting media 20

Powderpuff (*Calliandra haematocephala*) 32, 104, 105, 106

Powderpuff, Dwarf Red
   (*Calliandra haematocephala* 'Nana') 32

Prickly-Pear Cactus (*Opuntia* spp.) 63, 105, 106, 107

Princess-Flower (*Tibouchina* spp.) 9, 15, 78, 98, 104, 106

Privet, Florida (*Forestiera segregata*) 46, 96

Privet, Japanese (*Ligustrum japonicum*) 57

Privet, Variegated Chinese
   (*Ligustrum sinense* 'Variegatum') 57

pruning 7, 9, 10, 17-19, 95-103

pruning wounds   19, 98

Psychotria nervosa   68

Purple Anise   (*Illicium floridanum*)   53

pyracantha   68, 96-97

Pyracantha coccinea   68

Q

Queen Sago   (*Cycas circinalis*)   40, 105

Queen's Crape Myrtle   8

R

rain gauge   87

Raphiolepis indica   68

Raphiolepis umbellata   69

Red Bottlebrush   (*Callistemon citrinus*)   33, 104, 105, 106

Red-Edged Dracaena   (*Dracaena marginata*)   43, 105

Red-Tip Photinia   4, 19

Red Stopper   (*Eugenia rhombea*)   45, 104, 105, 107

Reeve's Spiraea   (*Spiraea cantoniensis*)   75, 105, 106

Rhapidophyllum hystrix   69

Rhapis excelsa   69

Rhododendron canescens   70

Rhododendron 'Fashion'   70

Rhododendron 'George Taber'   70

root
    ball   19, 85
    development   22
    system   19, 87
    zone   19, 88, 90

root-bound   19

rose   98

Rose-of-Sharon   (*Hibiscus syriacus*)   6, 7, 50, 104, 105, 106

Round-Leaf Hawthorn   (*Raphiolepis umbellata*)   9, 69, 105, 106

Royal Fern   (*Osmunda regalis*)   63, 104, 107

run-off
    fertilizer   86, 94-95
    rainwater   11

Russelia equisetiformis   71

S

Sage, Texas   (*Leucophyllum frutescens*)   56

Sago, King   (*Cycas revoluta*)   41

Sago, Queen   (*Cycas circinalis*)   40

salt tolerance   25, 26-83

Sanchezia   (*Sanchezia* spp.)   71, 106, 107

Sanchezia spp.   71

Sandankwa Viburnum   (*Viburnum suspensum*)   80, 104, 105

Sansevieria trifasciata   71

Saw Palmetto   (*Serenoa repens*)   6, 9, 73, 105, 107

Scaevola   (*Scaevola frutescens*)   9, 72, 104, 105, 107

Scaevola frutescens   72

Scaevola plumieri   72

scales   18

Schaefferia frutescens   72

Schefflera arboricola   73

Schefflera, Dwarf   (*Schefflera arboricola*)   73

Sea-Lavender   (*Mallotonia gnaphalodes*)   58, 105, 107

Sedge, Umbrella   (*Cyperus alternifolius*)   41

sediment   11

Selloum   (*Philodendron selloum*)   8, 65, 105, 106

Senna   (*Senna polyphylla*)   73, 105

Senna polyphylla   73

Serenoa repens   73

Seven-Year Apple   (*Casasia clusiifolia*)   35, 104, 105, 107

Severinia buxifolia   74

Shellflower, Variegated   (*Alpinia zerumbet* 'Variegata')   28

Shell Ginger, Variegated
    (*Alpinia zerumbet* 'Variegata')   28

Shower-of-Gold   (*Galphimia glauca*)   47

Shrimp Plant   (*Justicia brandegeana*)   55, 106, 107

Shrimp Plant, Golden   (*Pachystachys lutea*)   64

shrub
    arrangement   4. *See also* landscape designing
    establishment   85, 86, 91
    form   17, 96
    planting   21-23
    rejuvenation   101-102
    selection   4-12, 14-20, 24-83
    size   10, 11, 17, 96. *See also* shrub selection

Shrub-Althea   (*Hibiscus syriacus*)   50

shrubs, spring-flowering   97

Silver-Bush   (*Sophora tomentosa*)   74

Silver Buttonwood   7

Silver Grass, Japanese   (*Miscanthus sinensis*)   60

Silverleaf   (*Leucophyllum frutescens*)   56

Silverthorn   (*Elaeagnus pungens*)   44, 104, 105

Simpson's Stopper   (*Myrcianthes fragrans*)   61, 104, 105, 107

site assessment   4-12, 17

Small Anise   (*Illicium parviflorum*)   53

Snake Plant   (*Sansevieria trifasciata*)   71, 105, 107

Snowball, Tropical   (*Dombeya* spp.)   43

Snowbush   (*Breynia disticha*)   30, 104, 105, 106

soil
    acidic   15, 90
    alkaline   15
    amendments   23
    conditioners   22
    moisture   26-83
    pH   15, 26-83, 91
    sample, composite   91
    sensor   90
    testing   91

Sophora tomentosa   74

Southern Bayberry   (*Myrica cerifera*)   61

Southern Magnolia   8, 97

Southern Wax-myrtle   (*Myrica cerifera*)   61, 104, 107

Spanish Bayonet   (*Yucca aloifolia*)   6, 81, 105, 106, 107

Spanish Dagger   (*Yucca gloriosa*)   82, 105, 106, 107

Spanish Stopper   (*Eugenia foetida*)   44, 104, 105, 107

Spartina bakeri   74

Spiceberry   (*Eugenia rhombea*)   45

Spicewood   (*Calyptranthes pallens*)   34, 104, 105, 107

Spider-Lily, Giant   (*Crinum* x *amabile*)   39

spider mites   18

spirea 7, 75, 97-98
Spiraea cantoniensis 75
Spiraea, Reeve's (*Spiraea cantoniensis*) 75
spoke-jets 89
spokes 89
spray-jets 89
sprinkler systems
    hose-end 88-90
    in-ground 88
Star Magnolia (*Magnolia kobus* var. *stellata*) 58, 106
Star and Saucer Magnolia 98
stem rot 23
Stopper, Red (*Eugenia rhombea*) 45
Stopper, Simpson's (*Myrcianthes fragrans*) 61
Stopper, Spanish (*Eugenia foetida*) 44
Strelitzia reginae 75
String-Lily (*Crinum americanum*) 39, 104, 106, 107
Strobilanthes dyeranus 75
Sugarberry 9
Suriana maritima 76
Surinam Cherry (*Eugenia uniflora*) 45, 96, 104, 105
Swamp-Lily (*Crinum americanum*) 39
Sweet Osmanthus (*Osmanthus fragrans*) 63, 104, 105
Sweet Viburnum (*Viburnum odoratissimum*) 9, 80, 104, 105, 106
Sweetshrub (*Calycanthus floridus*) 33, 104, 105, 106, 107
Syzygium paniculatum 76

tabebuia 8
Tabernaemontana divaricata 76
Tea-Olive (*Osmanthus fragrans*) 63
Tecoma stans 77
Tecomaria capensis 77
temperature
    freezing 14-15, 20
    minimum winter 14-15
Tender Fountain Grass (*Pennisetum setaceum*) 64, 105, 106, 107
Ternstroemia gymnanthera 77
Ternstroemia, Japanese (*Ternstroemia gymnanthera*) 77
Tetrazygia bicolor 78
Tetrazygia, Florida (*Tetrazygia bicolor*) 78
Texas Sage (*Leucophyllum frutescens*) 56, 104, 105, 106
thinning 99-102
Thorny Elaeagnus (*Elaeagnus pungens*) 44
Thryallis (*Galphimia glauca*) 47, 98, 104, 106
Thunbergia erecta 78
Ti Plant (*Cordyline terminalis*) 38
Tibouchina spp. 78
time clock 87, 90
topiary 96
'Torulosa' Juniper
    (*Juniperus chinensis* 'Torulosa') 55, 105
Trailing Lantana 6, 7, 9
Tree Ligustrum 6
Tripsacum dactyloides 79

Tripsacum floridana 79
Tropical Hibiscus (*Hibiscus rosa-sinensis*) 50, 104, 10
Tropical Snowball (*Dombeya* spp.) 43, 106
Trumpet-Flower, Yellow (*Tecoma stans*) 77
Trumpet-Tree, Angel's (*Brugmansia* spp.) 30
Turk's Cap (*Malvaviscus arboreus*) 59, 104, 105, 106
Turnera ulmifolia 79
Twinberry (*Myrcianthes fragrans*) 61

U

Umbrella Sedge (*Cyperus alternifolius*) 41, 104

V

Variegated Caribbean Agave
    (*Agave angustifolia* 'Marginata') 27, 105, 107
Variegated Chinese Privet
    (*Ligustrum sinense* 'Variegatum') 57, 104, 105
Variegated Ginger 6
Variegated Pittosporum
    (*Pittosporum tobira* 'Variegata') 66, 104, 105
Variegated Shellflower
    (*Alpinia zerumbet* 'Variegata') 28, 104, 106
Variegated Shell Ginger
    (*Alpinia zerumbet* 'Variegata') 28
Varnish Leaf (*Dodonaea viscosa*) 42, 104, 105, 107
Viburnum obovatum 80
Viburnum odoratissimum 80
Viburnum suspensum 80
Viburnum tinus 81
Viburnum, Laurestinus (*Viburnum tinus*) 81
Viburnum, Sandankwa (*Viburnum suspensum*) 80
Viburnum, Sweet (*Viburnum odoratissimum*) 9, 80
Viburnum, Walter (*Viburnum obovatum*) 80
Vitex agnus-castus 81

W

Walter Viburnum (*Viburnum obovatum*) 80
watering 85-90
water ring, soil berm 22
Wax Mallow (*Malvaviscus arboreus*) 59
wax-myrtle 61, 97-98
Wax-myrtle, Southern (*Myrica cerifera*) 61
weeds 20-21, 23
Weeping Fig (*Ficus benjamina*) 46, 104, 105
whiteflies 18
Wild Cinnamon (*Canella winterana*) 34
Wild-Coffee (*Psychotria nervosa*) 68, 104, 105, 107
Winter Cinnamon (*Canella winterana*) 34, 104, 105, 106, 107
Wintergreen Barberry (*Berberis julianae*) 29, 104, 105, 106, 107

Y

Yaupon Holly 6, 107
Yaupon Holly, Dwarf
    (*Ilex vomitoria* 'Schilling's Dwarf') 7, 53, 96
Yedda Hawthorn (*Raphiolepis umbellata*) 69
Yellow-Alder (*Turnera ulmifolia*) 79, 106, 107
Yellow Butterfly Palm 7

Yellow-Elder (*Tecoma stans*) 77, 106

Yellow Poinciana 6

Yellow Trumpet-Flower (*Tecoma stans*) 77

Yesterday-Today-and-Tomorrow
   (*Brunfelsia grandiflora*) 31, 105, 106

Yew, Japanese (*Podocarpus macrophyllus*) 67

Yew Podocarpus (*Podocarpus macrophyllus*) 67, 104,
   105

Yucca aloifolia 81

Yucca filamentosa 82

Yucca gloriosa 82

Yucca, Aloe (*Yucca aloifolia*) 81

Yucca, Filamentose (*Yucca filamentosa*) 82

Yucca, Mound-Lily (*Yucca gloriosa*) 82

Z

Zamia floridana 82

Zamia furfuracea 83